COMPLETE STARTER GUIDE TO
Making
Wooden Boxes

Learn to Craft Beautiful and Practical Containers for Everyday Use

ALBERT KLEINE

FOX CHAPEL
PUBLISHING

© 2025 by Albert Kleine and Fox Chapel
Publishing Company, Inc.
Complete Starter Guide to Making Wooden Boxes
is an original work, first published in 2025 by Fox
Chapel Publishing Company, Inc. The patterns
contained herein are copyrighted by the author.
Readers may make copies of these patterns for
personal use. The patterns themselves, however,
are not to be duplicated for resale or distribution
under any circumstances. Any such copying is a
violation of copyright law.

ISBN 978-1-4971-0504-1

The Cataloging-in-Publication Data is on file with
the Library of Congress.

Managing Editor: Gretchen Bacon

Acquisitions Editor: Kaylee J. Schofield

Editor: Joseph Borden

Designer: Mike Deppen

Proofreader and Indexer: Kelly Umenhofer

To learn more about the other great books from
Fox Chapel Publishing, or to find a retailer near
you, call toll-free 800-457-9112.
Send mail to:
903 Square Street
Mount Joy, PA 17552
or visit us at *www.FoxChapelPublishing.com*.

We are always looking for talented authors. To
submit an idea, please send a brief inquiry to
acquisitions@foxchapelpublishing.com.

Printed in China
First printing

Introduction

Making boxes presents two huge advantages to the beginner hobbyist woodworker: 1) boxes are generally small projects that can be completed in short time spans, and 2) since they are usually small, the cost of materials is generally low. So, when I started my woodworking journey, instead of throwing all of my free time (and disposable income) into a couple of large projects, I chose to focus on boxes as my entry point into woodworking. It took me too long to figure this secret out, so I hope this book can spare you some of the time and effort.

When I first decided to jump into woodworking over a decade ago, I had absolutely no idea where to begin. As someone with no formal education in the craft, the variety and breadth of subjects under the general umbrella of "woodworking" was daunting. I also wanted to make sure that my time was well spent. I was intent on becoming well-rounded, and that meant taking on projects that would further my skill set. With a full-time job and intentions of starting a family, I needed to make sure all my shop time was productive.

After wandering aimlessly from project to project with no direction (my early work truly is quite bad), I eventually realized the value of focusing on boxes for my woodworking education. I found that making numerous and varied boxes—each one introducing new techniques and styles—has helped me become a well-rounded woodworker. I was able to learn many different joinery methods, how to turn on a lathe, how to effectively resaw lumber, and much more, all with limited money and time.

Further, since the time and money investment in box-making is so low, it encourages experimentation. Even if you take a leap that ends up not working, the pain of starting over is minimal. And the payoff of discovering a new technique or design aspect to incorporate into your work is thrilling. Making boxes introduced me to carving, string inlay, marquetry, and many other techniques that I truly don't think I would have explored otherwise. This has helped me immensely in developing my own signature style instead of just copying the work of others.

This book is an attempt to put my own journey with box-making into print. We'll start with an in-depth look into joinery, the basic building block of any wooden box. Obtaining a solid foundation in joinery is absolutely essential if you intend on making your own boxes, so make sure you spend a lot of time getting comfortable here. From there, we'll move on to the box-making itself.

The projects are arranged roughly in order of difficulty—the first is one that a beginner should be able to pick up quickly, and the last few are for more seasoned woodworkers. As you progress through making the boxes, you'll pick up essential skills that can be applied in numerous other woodworking projects. And while this book is primarily focused around the projects, the techniques are presented in such a way that it can act as a reference that you'll employ throughout your woodworking career.

My hope is that, by the end, you will feel comfortable applying the techniques you learned here to your own box designs and move away from relying on project plans. In that vein, I've tried to keep the projects as straightforward as possible—you should feel free to experiment and add your own imprint whenever you feel comfortable!

12

16

34

102

64

114

120

Table of Contents

48

72

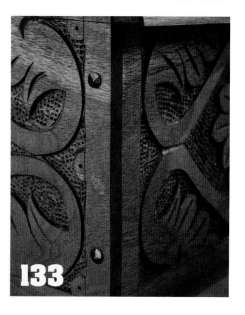

133

Getting Started

Before delving into discussions on joinery and box-making itself, it's important to get organized, prepared, and have a working knowledge of the tools and materials you'll be handling. Knowing what you need, how to use it, and having it readily available will make your shop time much more productive and allow you to focus all your attention on your projects. This chapter is meant to provide general advice on how to go about doing that.

Preparation and Safety

The best way to start any box-making project is to assemble all your materials prior to starting. This is important not only for the sake of efficiency, but also for ensuring your box-making is a success. Running around trying to gather the things you need while working can quickly put you in a headspace that simply isn't going to produce good work. Do yourself a personal favor and gather everything in the project materials list before you attempt anything—you'll thank me later.

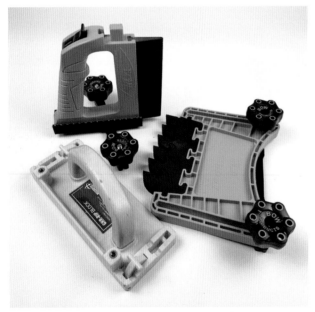

An example of auxiliary safety devices available: featherboards and push blocks. These are vital for keeping your hands and fingers away from sharp, fast-moving blades.

Another extremely important part of preparing for any woodworking project is safety. Woodworking is a wonderful hobby that can unfortunately leave you with devastating injuries very quickly if you are not attentive. Always make sure to outfit yourself with proper PPE whenever in the shop—dust masks, ear protection, and eye protection are a must when working with any power tools. Additionally, many power tools have safety guards installed on them and the ability to expose only the amount of a cutter that you need (e.g. you can drop the blade guard on a band saw to just above your stock to avoid catastrophe if the blade breaks). Learn how to use these safety features before using the tool—and never remove them, even if that "expert" on YouTube says it's fine.

Safety concerns don't go away when the power tools go off. Speaking from experience, it's very easy to hurt yourself quite badly with a hand tool. One thing I've found helpful is to constantly be aware of where both of my hands are whenever using a hand tool. My friend and fellow woodworker Vic Tesolin often says to make sure there's no "meat" in the path of a cutting edge. Beginners will often use a tool like a chisel with one hand, leaving the other vulnerable to the sharp edge should the chisel slip or wood break unexpectedly. Staying focused, present, and mindful is key to avoiding injury when using hand tools.

There are, of course, improvements you can make to your shop to ensure it remains injury free. Investing money in good dust collection will not only make your work safer by keeping your space clean, but your lungs will also thank you in the long term. Additionally, plenty of manufacturers make add-on safety devices like featherboards, push sticks, and jigs that I find also make my work much more accurate.

The point here is that safety should not be considered an afterthought in woodworking; it's an active process that requires you to be mindful about every task you are completing. Mitigate risks with proper equipment and training, and if something feels unsafe to you, don't risk it!

Materials

All the projects in this book use solid wood as the main box material. Solid wood is not dimensionally stable. Fluctuations in humidity and temperature can cause already prepared boards to bow, cup, or twist. This is a particular concern when a box lid is just a free-floating piece of wood. Nothing is preventing that board from going all out of whack! Milling your stock ahead of time to the listed project dimensions and allowing the wood to acclimate to your shop will save you a ton of headaches when it comes time to actually work with your stock. You'll notice in the projects that I occasionally make a comment about wood species or type of stock (quartersawn, flatsawn, riftsawn, etc.) to help mitigate wood movement concerns—these are born of experience so take note.

Sourcing decent hardwood lumber can be a chore depending on your local area. Woodworking stores typically stock pre-milled lumber, but the lack of variety and high prices make them not the best option. Connect with local woodworkers in your area to find out who the good suppliers are, as they can be hard to find through simple internet searches. It's also a good idea to establish a good relationship with your supplier. My main source—Alexander Brothers in Timberville, Virginia—regularly sets aside stock for me because they know the work that I do and my

A Note on Wood Selection

One of the most overlooked aspects of woodworking for beginners is the wood itself. I deeply encourage readers to educate themselves on the basic properties of wood through both research and experimentation, using resources like *Understanding Wood* by R. Bruce Hoadley—a must-read for anyone interested

An example of straight-grained, quartersawn lumber. Shown here are Douglas fir, Sitka spruce, and cherry.

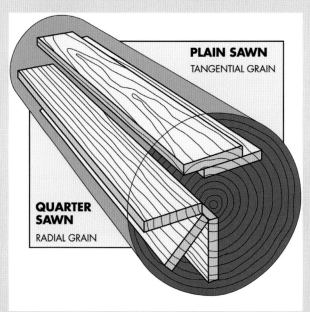

Plain- or flat-sawn wood is cut directly through the log, maximizing material usage and displaying attractive patterns with minimal defects. Quartersawn and rift-sawn wood offer greater stability and distinctive grain features, making them ideal for furniture.

in woodworking. When making boxes, which are typically small items, I prefer using straight-grained wood, like rift or quartersawn, for its stability and clean appearance. This choice allows me to employ techniques that are usually risky in woodworking, such as gluing a quartersawn board directly to the bottom of a box without concern for cracking. Furthermore, it's always worth investing a bit more in high-quality lumber. Early in my career, I learned that cheap wood not only costs in terms of quality but also wastes precious time.

material preferences. This saves me a ton of time and hassle when gathering materials for a project.

In addition to solid wood, some of the projects also use plywood. When sourcing plywood, try to use Baltic birch, if possible. The quality compared to big box store plywood is unmatched, and it's easy enough to get at a specialty woodworking store or online retailer.

Shop Supplies

Having a steady supply of consumables on hand is essential for a well-functioning shop. The last thing you want is unnecessary downtime because you don't have something you need to progress to the next step. Probably the most-used consumables in a woodworking shop are abrasives. I always make sure to have plenty of hook-and-loop sandpaper for my orbital sander, in addition to standard sheets for any hand sanding. PSA-backed sandpaper sheets are also great to have around for making quick sanding blocks out of scraps of wood. In addition to sandpaper, very fine steel wool (or even synthetic steel wool) is an essential for final buffing of finishes.

Most of the projects in this book, and woodworking in general, use wood glue, so it's a

good idea to buy it in quantity. Titebond II is my preferred brand because of its short open time—the glue sets fairly quickly and allows me to progress without much downtime. If you think you'll need a bit more time to set things properly during a complex glue up, then Titebond III is a better option. On the flip side, using a good cyanoacrylate glue (also known as CA glue or superglue) with an accelerator is great for getting an immediate grab—just don't use it in heavily stressed areas.

You'll also want to make sure you have plenty of supplies on hand for cleanup. Shop rags and fine bristle brushes are necessary when doing a glue up, so don't skimp on them. Denatured alcohol, mineral spirits, and acetone are all readily available on the hardware store shelf and can be used to both dilute finishes (e.g. denatured alcohol is a solvent for shellac, mineral spirits for linseed oil) and clean up any messes.

Finishes

The vast array of finishes on the market, each with unique properties like appearance, durability, and longevity, can be daunting for both novices and experienced woodworkers. The complexities of these finishes are too extensive for a brief discussion here. In this book, I suggest using your preferred finish for the boxes, as the choice often depends on personal preferences and the desired outcome. For those starting out, here are some straightforward options:

Oil: One of the simplest and most appealing finishes for boxes is an oil finish. Options range from pure tung and boiled linseed oils to proprietary blends. I favor pure tung oil, diluted 50-50 with mineral spirits, applied with a lint-free rag. After wiping off any excess and allowing it to dry for at least 12 hours, I either apply another coat or lightly buff it with #0000 steel wool. For additional protection, you can add an oil-based polyurethane to the mix, combining all three components in equal parts for an easy-to-apply finish. *Note: Be sure to dispose of oil-soaked rags properly and according to the manufacturer's instructions, as they can spontaneously combust.*

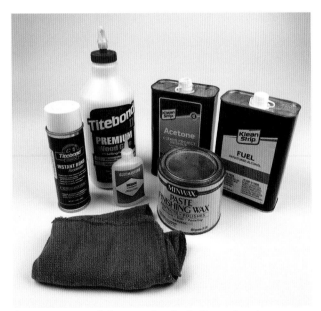

An assortment of shop staples, including solvents, rags, and finishes.

Lacquer:
Although not my favorite, many prefer lacquer for finishing boxes. It can be sprayed or wiped on, but spraying light coats is best to avoid accumulation in corners and on various surfaces. You can mix your own lacquer with thinner and use an HVLP system, or simply use a spray can from a hardware store.

Finishes, such as shellac, can create a smooth and appealing look to a box.

Shellac and Wax: I frequently use a one-pound cut of dewaxed shellac (one pound of shellac flakes per gallon of denatured alcohol) applied with a lint-free cotton rag. Light coats, buffed with steel wool between applications, create a fantastic finish. For additional sheen, a final buffed layer of paste wax can be applied. Before any glue-ups, I apply a washcoat of shellac to the interior parts to seal the grain, which prevents grain raising from glue squeeze-out and saves the hassle of re-sanding. Ensure the shellac is dewaxed if you plan to apply a different topcoat.

Other Materials

Everything listed so far should be viewed as necessities for general woodworking, but for box-making and the projects in this book specifically, some extra materials are needed.

Veneers are extremely common in box-making, usually to add some decorative element to a project that is not possible with solid wood. All the veneers used in the projects are ¹⁄₁₆" (1.6mm) thick, much thicker than standard commercial veneer. I use thicker veneers because not only are they far easier to use and handle than commercial veneers, but I can also saw them myself at the band saw using whatever stock I want. If you are uncomfortable sawing your own veneers or don't have a suitable band saw, finding ¹⁄₁₆" (1.6mm) thick veneer at a woodworking store or online is very easy.

A variety of paint is great to have on hand for adding a splash of color to your work. I like to use milk paint in my work (either true casein-based milk paint or acrylic imitations) due to ease of application, but I'll try anything. Perusing the paint aisle at my local art supply store introduced me to metallic, glitter, pearl, and other paint types that I've incorporated into my work countless times. Different paint types have wildly different effects that can be helpful in getting the look you are going for, so don't be afraid to experiment.

Similarly, fabrics and thick decorative paper are used extensively in box-making to line otherwise plain Baltic birch plywood panels. A small floral pattern can brighten up a box bottom easily, and all you need is a bit of spray adhesive. Craft supply and general merchandise stores have plenty of papers and fabric scraps for sale if you need them quickly, but if you are looking for an extensive variety, a dedicated fabric store is your best option.

Additional materials used in box-making, such as veneer, fabric, and decorative paints.

Tools

Other than available space, the biggest barrier to entry for any type of woodworking is the cost of tools. Woodworking is undoubtedly an expensive hobby, and if you plan on establishing a shop of your own, you should plan to spend a good bit of money getting set up.

I do want to note, however, that it is very easy to go down the path of thinking you need to own the absolute best of every single woodworking tool available. Spending money on quality tools is very rarely a bad idea, and it will save you a lot of frustration, but avoid the ever-present impulse to become a tool collector, and get the best tools you can afford. Remember that tool companies exist to sell products, and that something billed as an "essential" tool may not be so essential outside the world of marketing copy. If you are reading this book, you presumably want to be in the shop making things—try to keep the quantity, type, and quality of tools you are purchasing focused squarely on that goal.

Power Tools

The power tools required for box-making are pretty much the same ones needed for all woodworking projects. At the bare minimum, it's a good idea to have a jointer, planer, and band saw—these are workshop essentials. The jointer and planer are necessary for milling your own stock, and the band saw can take care of most cuts you'll need to do. A table saw is another helpful tool to have, but if you can only choose one, the band saw is a far better choice for its versatility. Not only can a band saw do most of the operations a table saw can (albeit leaving a surface that needs cleaning), but it can also resaw. Resawing can help you save a lot of material that would otherwise be planed away during thicknessing.

Another power tool that should be considered necessary in box-making is a router table. Since boxes are typically small, routing grooves with a handheld router can be both difficult and dangerous. I rout grooves in almost every box I make, so getting a decent router table with a variety of cutting bits was a no-brainer.

A band saw can be used for a variety of woodworking projects and is particularly useful in box-making.

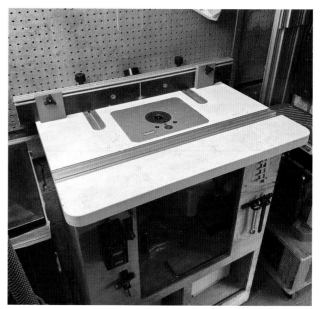

A router table is a vital tool for box-making, as it is often used to add grooves and other critical components.

A lathe isn't necessary for box-making, but it can be a handy tool. One project in this book is made entirely on the lathe.

A lathe is a great accessory tool to have in the workshop. While not strictly necessary for box making, having a lathe allows you to make your own pulls and other parts that can be used in your projects. Some of the projects in this book make use of one for just that reason, and one box is even made entirely on the lathe.

You don't need to get a full professional turner's kit to get started. A small benchtop lathe with a starter set of turning chisels, and a few other accessories (like a four jaw scroll chuck and drill chuck) are all you really need for the projects covered here.

You'll of course find yourself needing additional power tools as you continue working, but most of these can be picked up on the cheap as you go. A drill press, power drill, dust extractor, palm router, and random orbital sander should all be on your wish list for box-making, but don't feel the need to grab something until you need it. And always remember that there are multiple ways of doing

things—power tools can be stationary and take up a lot of space, so think long and hard about whether or not you really need to give up potentially limited real estate for that machine you've been eyeing.

Hand Tools

As you work through the projects in this book, you'll notice that there is a strong focus on using hand tools. The main reason for this is box-making is a very precise task. Saws, planes, and chisels, when used properly, can give you much more accuracy and control than power tools. Hand tools also allow you to slowly sneak up on cuts and make slight alterations so that everything comes together seamlessly.

There are thousands upon thousands of woodworking hand tools, so assembling your first kit can be extremely confusing. Just like with power tools, your work and preferences will dictate what you end up needing, but here's a list of my personal must-haves to get you started:

The three most important planes: (from left to right) a smoothing plane, a block plane, and a shoulder plane.

Smoothing plane. I use a Stanley No. 3 or No. 4. This is used to "smooth" wood by taking light shavings. It's also used as a general-purpose plane that can do pretty much any planing task.

Block plane. This is used primarily as a small trimming plane. It's also used for adding chamfers and trimming small parts.

Shoulder plane. This is a plane where the blade extends across the entire sole, allowing shavings to be taken in corners—a must for cleaning up rabbets.

Dovetail saw. This is a rip-filed backsaw used to make fine cuts for joinery.

Coping/fret saw. This is used primarily to remove waste between tails and pins in dovetails. Deep throat fret saws are also used in marquetry.

Flush cut saw. This is a flexible, spineless saw that is used to cut materials flush to a reference surface.

Set of bench chisels. These are the workhorses of the shop. Your bench chisels will be used in almost every single woodworking project you'll ever do, so do your research and spend wisely.

Carving gouges. These are chisels with curved or angled edges and are used to do detailed carvings in wood.

Mallet. This is used to assemble joints, pound chisels, and any other number of "whacking" tasks in the shop. I prefer the round "carver's" versions over the square "joiner's" ones.

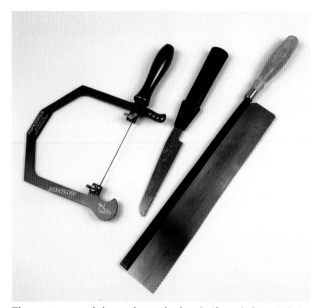

Three saws used throughout the book: (from left to right) a fret/coping saw, dovetail saw, and flush cut saw.

An assortment of marking tools: (from left to right) a marking gauge, awl, marking knife, and combination square.

Marking gauge. This is used to mark reference lines when cutting joinery. I prefer the modern, wheel-style marking gauges over more traditional knife ones.

Marking knife. Used to establish lines for joinery. A marking knife is essential for precisely layout, as a pencil will leave lines that are simply too thick.

Combination square. This is used to measure and transfer lines and check for square. A good combination square is invaluable in the woodworking shop—get a good one.

Awl. This is used to mark starting holes for drill bits. The divot left by an awl helps keep the drill bit from wandering and lets you more precisely locate holes.

A standard set of chisels and carving gouges.

When it comes to buying hand tools, it's best to avoid anything off the shelf at a hardware or big box store. Most of these tools (particularly the hand planes) are simply not made well enough for fine box-making. Luckily, antiques of the tools listed in this section are generally well made and easy to come by. With a bit of refurbishing, flea market finds can be great—just be ready to put in a little effort to get things working properly. Of course, you can always

buy new hand tools, but make sure they are suitable for fine woodworking. The premium brands (Lie Nielsen, Veritas, etc.) make fantastic planes, and if your budget is a little lighter, high-quality imports (Woodriver, Melbourne Tool Company) will get the job done just fine.

Other hand tools you'll need are what I put under the banner of "general shop tools." Things like wrenches, screwdrivers, clamps, and other common items are important for a shop. Most of these items are probably already kicking around your garage, and you'll pick them up as your work dictates, so an exhaustive list isn't necessary.

Jigs

In addition to materials and tools, you'll also need a few basic jigs to get started with the projects in this book.

Shooting boards are a great way to use a hand plane to trim the ends of boards (and even the long grain edges of boards in some cases). They allow you to sneak up on the exact fit of box components, and as we'll see in later chapters, they can even be used

A mitered shooting board (right) and standard shooting board (left).

to cut joinery. I repeatedly use two shooting boards throughout this book: a simple 90-degree shooting board and a mitered shooting board. These jigs have become essentials in my shop and get used on almost every project.

The shooting board plans in the back of the book take only a few pieces of plywood and an afternoon to complete, but they'll save you a ton of time and hassle in the shop. While the projects can be completed without them, I strongly encourage you to take the time to incorporate shooting boards into your woodworking.

Tips for Building Shooting Boards

The plans for the shooting boards are fairly self-explanatory, but there are some tips that can make the process go much more smoothly.

90-Degree Shooting Board

1. **1. Cut all plywood and solid wood to listed dimensions.** Drill and countersink holes in the top and screw it to the base. While you have your drill or drill press out, you can also drill holes in the fence and attach the cleat.

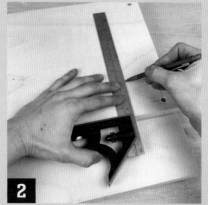
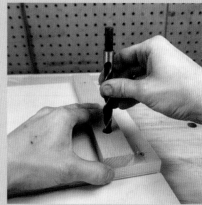

2. Place a combination square against the edge of the shooting board top. Then, strike a line about 2" (5.1cm) from the top edge. Align the edge of the fence with the pencil line, and make sure it's just a bit proud of the edge the plane is used against. Use ¼" (6mm) and ½" (13mm) drill bits in the corresponding fence holes to mark drilling locations on the shooting board top.

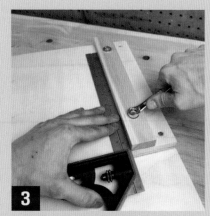

3. Drill and install threaded inserts in the shooting board top. Attach the fence with bolts and washers, using a combination square to keep the fence square to the edge of the shooting board top.

4. Make a test cut on the shooting board by placing the stock firmly against the fence. Position a hand plane on its side and plane the endgrain of the stock. Check to see if the end you planed is square to the edges of the board. If your stock is out of square, loosen the right bolt on the shooting board fence, pivot the fence in the appropriate direction, and tighten the bolt. Continue adjusting and checking until your stock is square.

Miter Shooting Board

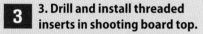

1. Cut all plywood and solid wood to listed dimensions. Note that the shooting board top has a bevel cut on the side next to the ramp—don't worry about getting this at exactly 45 degrees. Drill and countersink holes in the top and screw it to the base. While you have your drill or drill press out, you can also drill holes in the fence, the underside of the shooting board base, the spacer, and the cleat.

3. Drill and install threaded inserts in shooting board top. Attach fence with bolts and washers, using a combination square to keep the fence square to the edge of the shooting board top.

4. Prepare stock for the shooting board ramp. It should be 1 ¾" (4.5cm) thick and at least 2 ½" (6.4cm) wide (I go wider if possible) to make the bevel cut easy. Set a table saw blade to 45 degrees or a band saw table to 45 degrees, and set the fence so that the resulting cut will yield a 2" (5.1cm) wide ramp. Cut the ramp from the blank.

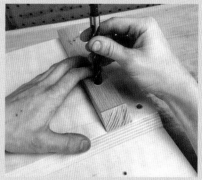

2. Place a combination square against the edge of the shooting board top. Then, strike a line about 2" (5.1cm) from the top edge. Align the edge of the fence with the pencil line and make sure it's just a bit proud of the edge the plane is used against. Use ¼" (6mm) and ½" (13mm) drill bits in the corresponding fence holes to mark drilling locations on the shooting board top.

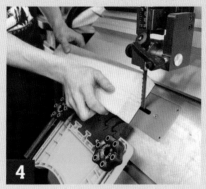

5. Prepare the ramp for planing. It's very likely that your ramp will not be exactly 45 degrees. Attach an F-clamp to the ends of the ramp and tighten the clamp body into a vise, so the face of the ramp your plane will ride against is facing up.

6. Using a smoothing or jack plane, plane the ramp. Check repeatedly with a combination square against the base of the ramp. You want to take your time here, and ensure the ramp is exactly 45 degrees across its entire length. This can be a tedious process, but stick with it—you'll only have to do this once!

8. When using the shooting board, make sure you are placing firm pressure on the plane against the ramp. As long as the ramp is exactly 45 degrees relative to its base, this will result in a perfect miter cut. Follow the same steps in the 90-degree shooting board tips to test for a square cut, and adjust if necessary.

7. Place the ramp against the edge of the shooting board top and clamp it into place. Drill screws into the ramp through the underside of the shooting board. Remove the clamps and screw in the cleat on the underside of the board and the spacer on the right side of the ramp.

Joinery

A book on box-making essentials would be incomplete without an in-depth discussion of joinery. After all, at its core, a box is just four boards of wood joined together with a top and bottom. Getting a good foundation in joinery is absolutely necessary if you want to make boxes, and it will help you immensely as you continue in your woodworking. That's why before we go into the projects, we're going to take some time and focus directly on the topic.

So, what is joinery? It's basically exactly what it sounds like. Joinery is the term woodworkers use to describe the method by which two pieces of wood are joined together. How that is done can be achieved in any number of ways—with adhesives, fasteners, interlocking wood parts, or any combination of methods.

In this chapter, we'll go over some of the most common and useful joints used in box-making, progressing in difficulty as we go.

From top to bottom: pinned butt joint, rabbet joint, miter joint, dovetail joint, half-blind dovetail joint.

Getting familiar with these joints early on is essential for completing the projects presented in this book, so make sure you spend the time and effort necessary to really master them.

Some of the joints you may find exceedingly simple, while others can take quite a bit of time to get the hang of. As with most things in life, the way to get good at them is by practicing. It's a good idea to spend some time just attempting to make a successful joint before moving on to a full project.

And try not to get discouraged if your first few attempts at the more challenging joints are less than perfect. I can't possibly count the number of sad, gap-and-crack laden dovetail joints I put together before getting comfortable with them.

Different joints have different properties that make them more suitable in some circumstances than others. A miter joint, for instance, is a great option for a small jewelry box, but would be potentially disastrous if used on a drawer. That's why, in addition to showing you how to actually do the joint, we'll discuss the pros and cons of each method.

By the end of this chapter, you should have a solid understanding of box-making joints, how to do them, and their relative advantages. The joints are presented here primarily so you can complete the projects in this book, but they can also serve as a reference for any project you may take on later. My hope is you'll gain the knowledge, skills, and confidence to employ these joints in all of your woodworking.

Butt Joint

Undoubtedly the simplest joint you can use on a box, butt joints are achieved when the ends of two boards

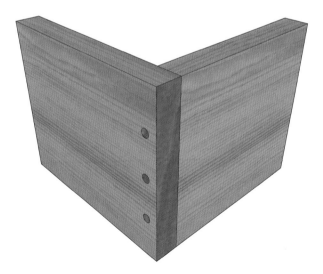

A rendering of a simple butt joint. Useful for when you need a quick and easy joint. Butt joints are simply the edges of two boards "butted" up against each other. Dowels, screws, or nails are typically used to strengthen the joint, as any glue here is of little use.

are "butted" up against each other. Even though they are very simple, they serve as a good example to bring up some key considerations in box-making.

The thing about butt joints is that they aren't really joints in themselves—they need something additional to actually hold everything together. Probably the most common way of securing a butt joint is by driving screws or nails through the face of one board and into the endgrain of the other. Dowels, biscuits, and dominoes are other common options.

Regardless of the method used, it's important to know why a butt joint can't be held together with just glue. There's no need to get into the details, but just remember this: glue on endgrain will not result in a reliable joint. Since a butt joint has endgrain touching long grain, any glue applied here is of little structural use. It might hold the joint together temporarily, but eventually it will fail.

How to Make a Butt Joint Overview

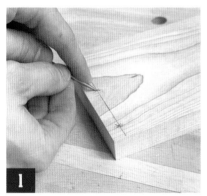

1. Start with two pieces of square stock, and on one, mark the location for the dowel pins. Make sure these are centered in the board they are entering—for example, if your stock is ¾" (19mm) thick, make a mark ⅜" (9.5mm) from the edge of the board. The number of pins depends on the width of your board. Choose a number and evenly space them along the width of the board. After marking with a pencil, make indentations with an awl.

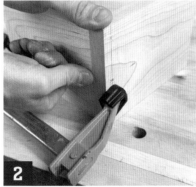

2. Spread a bead of wood glue along the endgrain of another piece of scrap. Butt it up against the other and clamp the boards together. Spend time making sure that everything here is aligned, using your fingers to feel for any proud wood at the joints. Let the joint sit for about 30 minutes so the glue has time to set temporarily.

3. Using a ¼" (6mm) drill bit (adjust size accordingly for different stock thicknesses), drill straight into the marks you made. Drill as straight as possible. Putting a combination square on your workpiece as a visual reference can help. Make sure you drill about 2" (5.1cm) or so into the mating board.

4. Cut some dowel stock a bit longer than the holes you drilled, coat them in wood glue, and pound them into the holes. After about 30 minutes, trim the dowels with a flush cut saw, and clean up the joint surface with a hand plane or some sandpaper affixed to a sanding block.

Rabbet Joint

A rabbet joint isn't all that different from a butt joint, and the same general principles apply. It's an endgrain-to-long-grain joint, so glue alone isn't sufficient to keep it together. Still, there are some differences that give it an advantage over the butt joint.

Rabbet joints are made by cutting a notch—or rabbet—in the edge of a board. The mating board is then glued and (typically) pinned in the rabbet. The nice thing about a rabbet joint is it is very easy to keep things aligned when clamping, gluing, and pinning. The geometry of the joint keeps things in place.

Pinned rabbet joints are a good option for drawers when you don't have the time (or haven't yet developed the skills) to do half-blind dovetails. The pins provide mechanical strength to resist the forces put on the drawer by being opened and closed repeatedly.

A rendering of a rabbet joint. A more sophisticated version of the butt joint, a rabbet joint takes advantage of a small notch—or rabbet—cut in the edge of one board to provide mechanical strength. Like the butt joint, dowels are often used to provide additional strength. This is useful for when you want an uninterrupted drawer front, but don't have the time to do a half-blind dovetail.

How to Make a Rabbet Joint Overview

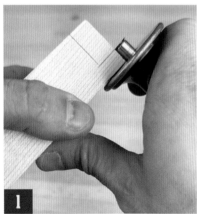

1. Start with two pieces of stock, one about ⅛"–¼" (3–6mm) thicker than the other. Set a marking gauge to the thickness of the thinner board, and on the thicker board, mark the location for the rabbet along the inside face and edges– this will help prevent tear-out at the router table by severing the wood fibers.

2. With a ½" (13mm) upcut spiral or straight flute cutter bit in your router, set the router table fence so that the cutter aligns with your marking gauge line. If your rabbet is wider than your router bit, first set the bit to remove slightly less material than the width of the bit and cut the rabbet. Then, repeat the process again with the bit set at your gauge line.

3. Don't try and rout the rabbet all in one go. It's not only dangerous but also risks ruining your entire project. Routers should always be viewed as finishing tools, not for bulk material removal. Take light passes, pushing your stock with a scrap block to avoid blowout at the exit of the cut. Raise the router bit by about 1/16"–⅛" (1.5–3.2mm) before each pass until you reach your final depth.

4. Spread a bead of glue along the inside of the rabbet and clamp the mating board in place. Use clamps in both directions to make sure the joint is fully closed. After the glue has had time to set, repeat the steps from the butt joint section to mark, drill, and trim pins.

Rabbet Pins

Depending on the project, you can choose which board of the rabbet joint receives pins. If you are making a drawer, its best to drill the pins so that they show on the board without the rabbet—this will keep the drawer front from falling off as it is opened and closed over a lifetime.

Miter Joint

The main benefit of the miter in box-making is aesthetic—it's only joint covered here that shows no visible endgrain. Just like butt and rabbet joints, glue alone here can be risky. The miter joint is mostly endgrain-to-endgrain contact, so don't expect the glue to hold in tough situations. Since miters are

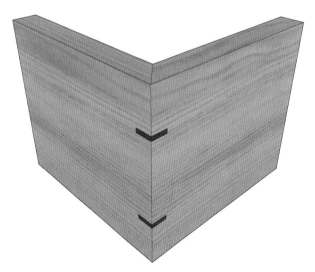

A rendering of a miter joint. Typically used in light-duty applications like small keepsake boxes, miter joints are a good option if you don't want any visible endgrain in your joint. Since the contact point between boards is mostly endgrain, though, the glue joint isn't particularly strong. Adding splines is a good idea if you think the extra strength will be needed, although I often skip them.

typically used in light-duty applications, however, some woodworkers opt to leave them alone and hope for the best. In situations when you need a little extra reinforcement, however, splines (thin strips of wood inserted into saw kerfs across the miter joint) can be added after the glue has set.

There are any number of ways to cut miters with both hand and power tools, but I've found the absolute best way to get a gapless joint is by using a mitered shooting board and hand plane. This removes all the hassle of fussing with angle settings on a table or miter saw. Once the board is built and dialed in, you can cut beautiful miters all day long without even thinking about it.

On page 15, I laid out plans for how to build and use a mitered shooting board—an absolutely essential tool in box-making that we'll use multiple times in the projects in this book. Let's go over how to use one and make a joint.

How to Make a Miter Joint Overview

1. Mark the inside faces of four box sides, making sure your pieces are square. Place a box side down on your mitered shooting board with the inside face facing up. Place a hand plane on the 45-degree ramp and begin planing the ends of the box side. Take light passes with the hand plane, making sure you are applying downward pressure against the 45-degree ramp.

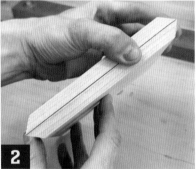

2. Continue checking the edge as you plane until you have just created a full 45-degree cut. Repeat on both ends of all four box sides. If you cut too much, don't panic—the only thing that really matters here is that opposing sides are the exact same length. Check opposing side lengths against each other, and make light plane passes where appropriate until they are equal.

3. Place all four box sides with the inside faces down and edges touching. It also helps to set up a straight edge to press the boards against and keep things in alignment. Stretch blue painter's tape across the joints, pulling tightly before you press down. You want the tape to have a bit of stretch to it as you close the joint.

4. Carefully turn all four sides over and lightly brush a 50/50 mixture of wood glue and water on all the miters. Allow to dry for about 10-30 minutes. This "glue size" will help seal the endgrain and ensure that the ensuing glue joint is much stronger.

5. Spread some wood glue on all the miters and fold the joints together carefully. If the tape is tight enough, you should feel the joints "snap" together as you bend them. Once all four corners are together, apply tape to the final joint and seal things up. On wider boards, you may want to add some strap clamps to tighten things up. Let the glue set and you're done!

Miter Joint Tips

Miters can be extremely frustrating to get right off the bat. A lot of people struggle with small gaps either on the inside or the outside of the joint. These issues are the result of two things: either your opposing sides are not of equal length, or your joints aren't exactly 45 degrees.

Continually check your miter with a combination square. Even if your shooting board is set up right, bad planing technique can give you angles that are slightly off. Make sure you are applying pressure against the 45-degree ramp as you plane—this is very important!

There are methods to somewhat fix gappy miters—like rolling the shaft of a screwdriver along the point of a miter to close it up—but these rarely give results that are fitting for a fine box. Taking the extra time to make sure everything is dialed in perfectly really is the best way to get a miter that both looks good and stays together.

One method for securing miters during glue-up is to use a strap clamp.

Through Dovetail

The through dovetail is a highly versatile and visually appealing joint that just so happens to be incredibly strong. Because of this, it is my favorite joint to use in box-making, and one that is essential to master if you want to get in the business of making fine boxes.

The strength of the dovetail comes from two sources. The first is mechanical. Note how the "tails" of one board fit perfectly into corresponding gaps in the opposing "pin" board. This is the first joint we've seen where one piece of wood is locking into another without the assistance of glue or fasteners.

The dovetail joint also has ample long grain-to-long grain wood contact. The sides of the tails and the pins (both long grain) touch each other directly, so any wood glue applied here is going to be incredibly strong. Together with the mechanical nature of the joint, once the glue dries on a dovetail, it simply isn't going to come apart without some serious destruction.

Of course, they take quite a bit of practice to get right, and many people are so intimidated by them that they never even try. After mastering the joint myself, I can say with absolute certitude that there is no magic trick or shortcut here. The way to get good at dovetails is to approach them with focus and purpose, and to cut a lot of practice joints.

Clear instructions and a lot of tips along the way can really speed things up. In this example, I am using stock that is 4⅝" (11.8cm) wide and ⅝" (16mm) thick. Any measurements referenced here are based on those dimensions, so if your stock is different, adjust measurements accordingly.

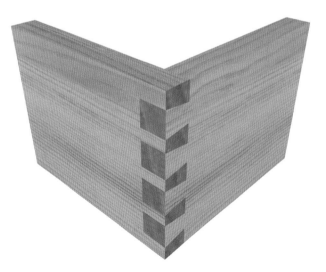

A rendering of a through dovetail. Even stronger than a box joint, a dovetail takes advantage of wedge-shaped joinery to provide a mechanical lock – the glue is just insurance here. Use when strength is absolutely necessary, or when you just want a very attractive looking joint that shows off your woodworking skills.

How to Make a Through Dovetail Overview

1. Gather two pieces of scrap, and set a marking gauge to project a bit more than the thickness of your stock. Scribe a line on the faces and edges of one board (the "tail board") and only on the face of the other (the "pin board").

2. Clamp the tail board in your vise with the end facing up. Draw a pencil line across the ends of the board about ¼" (6.4mm) from the edge. Set a pair of dividers to open 1⅜" (3.5cm) and place one point into a pencil mark. Set the other point into the board and make a mark. Rotate and "walk" the dividers along the edge of the board, making light marks with the points as you go.

3. Repeat this process, starting from the pencil mark at the other edge of the board. When you are finished, you should end up with four equally spaced marks. Use your combination square to extend pencil lines across these marks.

Spacing Dovetails

The distance between divider points in Step 2 is completely arbitrary. I chose that dimension because I knew it would yield three nicely spaced dovetails on the boards used in this example—and it didn't require any confusing math at all.

First, pick how many dovetails you want in your project, and set your dividers so that they are equal to about the width of what one tail would be. For example, if you chose four dovetails, open your dividers so they are about ¼ the width of your tail board. Place one point of the divider in a pencil line like Step 2, and walk along the board, except this time do not make any marks.

Count the number of "turns" you do with your dividers as you walk. This will be the number of dovetails on your project. The last "turn" is when the point of the divider goes past the pencil mark on the opposite end of the board. The distance between this pencil line and the point of the dividers is the pin width.

If you find that you aren't getting the number of tails you want, or the pin width is too small or large for your liking, simply open or close your dividers accordingly and start again. Once you have everything set, do the process laid out in steps 2 and 3, and you'll have nice and evenly spaced dovetails.

Measuring the distance between lines.

4. Set a bevel gauge to your desired dovetail angle. For this example, I chose seven degrees because it's a nice overall angle that provides adequate strength. Use the bevel gauge to transfer pencil lines to the face of your tail board down to the marking gauge line.

5. With the tail board clamped in your vise, place your saw directly on one of the lines. It is very important to ensure that your cut is square across the board here, so make sure you don't deviate from the guideline. Cuts that aren't perfectly square can cause problems later, so take your time.

6. Use the thumb and forefinger from your non-sawing hand as a fence to stabilize the saw on the line. Tilt the saw slightly to match the dovetail angle you drew on the face of the board. Once you feel comfortable that your saw is square across the board and tilted at approximately the correct angle, you are ready to cut.

7. Focus on holding the angle you set in the previous step while gently moving the saw forward and backward to establish a cut. The feel for this takes some time to build up, so practice on some scrap wood. Try not to put any downward pressure as you cut—the weight of the saw and gravity should be just enough to guide everything properly. Continue sawing, checking continually to make sure you aren't going past your marking gauge lines (especially on the side of the board that isn't facing you). Once you've reached your marking gauge line on both the front and the back of the board, your cut is complete.

8. Using a fret saw or coping saw, remove the waste between tails. Don't risk cutting into your baseline by getting too close here. The goal now is to remove the bulk of the waste, not all of it. Everything will be cleaned up later with a chisel.

Tips for Sawing

Cutting dovetails by hand can be intimidating, but luckily there are some tips and tricks that can make the whole process a lot easier

A nice thing about cutting dovetails is that the angle you cut them at really doesn't matter. Even if you wildly miss your pencil line, don't worry—you will automatically correct for it later when you mark your pins. Just make sure your cut is square across the board, and everything will be fine!

An example of all saw lines being done in one direction.

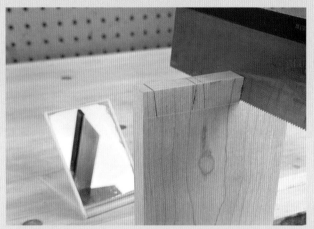

Using a mirror to check progress on the backside of the tail board.

If you are concerned about sawing past your marking gauge line (especially on the side of the board that you can't see), setting up a mirror on your bench to monitor progress is a good insurance policy.

Speaking of mirrors, you can use your saw plate's reflective properties to help you set up a cut. If your saw is square across the board, the edge of the board will reflect onto the saw plate in a straight line. If you aren't square, it will be kinked. Just check the reflection before you start sawing away!

When you first start out, getting comfortable with cutting on an angle can be tough. To make things easier, cut all your angles in one direction, then flip your board and cut your other marks. This will help you build up muscle memory for cutting the angle more quickly than trying to cut angles in both directions.

A dovetail guide will help you make perfect cuts.

If you just don't think you will be able to make a properly guided cut, there's no shame in using a dovetail guide. There are a number of great options on the market that ensure your cuts will come out perfectly. Even though I have personally cut thousands of dovetails by hand, I still regularly reach for my guide when I really need things to go just right.

Using the reflection on the saw plate to ensure your cuts are square.

9. Reorient the tail board in your vise so that the edge is facing up. Working from the waste side on the edge of the tail board, make a wedge shaped paring cut toward your marking gauge line. The result should be a small gullet in the waste side of the tail board that goes right up to the marking gauge line.

10. Place your saw in the gullet and make sure that it is square. Cut until you meet the dovetail angled cut that you made earlier. If the waste doesn't fall off easily, you may have to apply light pressure to snap it off. Any ugliness left behind can be cleaned up with a chisel. Remove the tail board from your vise and place it on your bench. Place a ¼" (6mm) chisel in the waste section between your tails. Make sure you don't get too close to your marking gauge line at first—try to stay about ⅛" (3mm) away.

11. Use a mallet to chop out waste. Only go about halfway through the board, or you'll risk blowout on the backside. As you chop, move your chisel closer and closer to your marking gauge line until about ¹⁄₃₂" (1mm) of waste remains.

12. Place your chisel directly in the marking gauge line. Angle your chisel so that it is slightly under 90 degrees—this will ensure that no lingering waste material keeps your joint from coming together. Deliver your final mallet blows, still making sure to only go halfway through the board.

13. Repeat steps 11 and 12 for all waste sections on both sides of the tail board. When doing final chops at the marking gauge line on the second side of the board, continue carefully until it meets the chop you made on the first side. The waste should then be easy enough to wrestle out between tails.

14. Clamp the tail board in your vise and clean up any remaining waste. It's important that any and all lingering waste be removed at this point, otherwise the joint won't come together later. Use whatever you have (chisels, marking knife, etc.) to make sure your tails are nice and clean.

15. Place a piece of blue painter's tape on the endgrain of your pin board and trim it with a knife. Clamp the pin board in your vise, and line up the tail board perpendicular over the end of the pin board. It can help to elevate your tail board with a hand plane so that everything lays flat.

16. With one hand placing firm downward pressure on the tail board, use a marking knife to "transfer" the walls of your tails onto the endgrain of the pin board. It helps to place your knife right up against the wall of the tail to act as a fence while you make your marks. Take your time here—accurate markings are critical for a successful joint!

Blue Painter's Tape and Pin Boards

I'm not exactly sure where I first saw the "blue tape method" for cutting dovetails, but it's commonly attributed to Mike Pekovich of *Fine Woodworking Magazine*. The blue painter's tape isn't really necessary at all, but it provides a nice visual cue to make sure you don't cut away too much material—as long as you leave the blue painter's tape unscathed, your joint should be fine.

I've also found that using the blue tape method allows me to get dovetail joints that fit almost perfectly right off the saw. When sawing my pin walls, I use the slight ridge created by the blue painter's tape to act as a fence for my saw. I just want the teeth of the saw slightly kissing the tape here—I certainly don't want to cut into it. Don't be afraid to get really close to the edge here—if you've gone too far, the tape will bunch up immediately as you start sawing and let you know you've gone too far!

Cut as close to the tape as possible.

Tips for Sawing Pins

When sawing tails, you want to make sure you are square across the endgrain relative to the face of the board. When sawing pins, you need to make sure you are sawing square to the edge of the board—i.e. there is no "tilt" to your saw like when you cut the tails. Use the pencil lines you transferred on the face of the board as a guide to saw straight—sawing on an angle can result in either a large gap or a cracked joint, so pay attention!

Aside from that, everything is the same! Remove the waste and chop to the base line just as you did on the tail board. Make sure you spend time ensuring that all lingering waste is removed.

When sawing pins, make sure you saw square to the edge of the board.

17. Remove the "tail" sections of the tape from the pin board. Transfer lines straight down from the edges of the tape to the baseline. This line will help you saw straight. The sections of the board where tape is missing are your waste sections. You want to remove all the material here. Following steps 13-14, remove the waste from the pin board.

18. After all the waste from the pin board has been removed, clamp it in your vise. Rub a pencil on the inside walls of your tails, and try to press the joint together by hand or with light mallet taps. Don't try to force the joint together! If it's too tight (which it probably will be!), pull the tail board out once you feel resistance.

19. The pencil markings from the tails will transfer to the walls of the pins where the joint is too tight. Using a chisel, pare lightly across the grain to remove these pencil markings from the pin walls. Re-pencil your tails and try to refit.

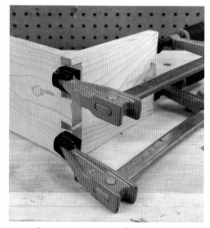

20. Keep refitting and paring until your joint comes together with moderate pressure. Once you are satisfied with a dry fit, spread glue on the walls of the pins and assemble and clamp the joint, placing pressure directly on the tails. Allow the glue to set.

21. After the glue has set, you'll notice your pins and tails are a bit proud. That's because of how you set your gauge all the way back in Step 1. Use a hand plane to level these out, planing in the direction of any small gaps. The blowout from planing will help fill them in and leave you with an attractive joint.

Half-Blind Dovetail

The half-blind dovetail really isn't all that different from the through dovetail. All the same principles about it being a strong joint apply, but the half-blind has one distinct advantage over the through dovetail. Since the tails don't go all the way through the pin board, the grain on the face of the pin board in half-blind dovetails remains uninterrupted. This makes it a perfect choice for drawer fronts (or any other situation) when you don't want any joinery to be visible.

The only difference in executing the joint is how you approach cutting the pin board (or in the case of half-blind dovetails, the "socket" board).

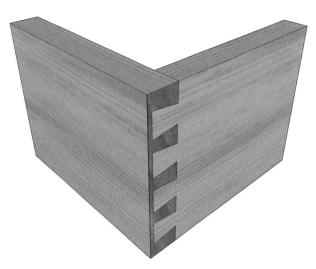

Very similar to the through dovetail, the half-blind dovetail provides the same strength, but with a board that isn't interrupted by visible joinery. It's the most challenging joint to execute of the joints presented here, but a must for drawers in high-end pieces.

How to Make a Half-Blind Dovetail Overview

1. To start, make sure your socket board is about ⅛"–¼" (3.2–6.4mm) thicker than your tail board. Set your marking gauge to the thickness of the pin board minus about ⅛" (3mm), and use this setting to mark the length of your tails on your tail board.

2. Mark and cut your tails. The steps for cutting a half-blind dovetail are exactly the same as for a through dovetail, until it comes time to cut and fit the pin board. To continue the example below, first do steps 1-14 in the previous section. We'll pick up from there.

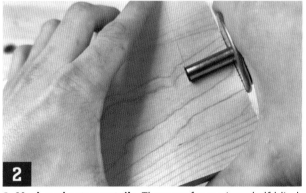

3. Set a marking gauge to the thickness of the tail board, and mark along the edge of the socket board. Place a piece of blue painter's tape on the endgrain of your socket board and trim it with a knife. Set your marking gauge to the length of your tails (the distance from the tip the tails to the baseline), and scribe a line along the endgrain of your socket board.

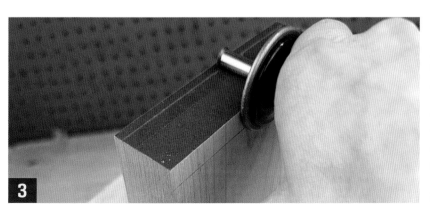

4. Clamp the socket board in your vise, and line up the tail board perpendicular over the end of the pin board. Unlike through dovetails, in which the ends of the tails lined up with the face of the pin board, line up the ends of the tails with the marking gauge line you made in the previous step.

5. Mark the location of your tails with a marking knife. Remove the tail board and the tail sections of the tape from the pin board. Just like in the through dovetail, the sections of the board where tape is missing are your waste sections. At this point, I also like to draw a pencil line straight down from the tape edges to the baseline and mark the waste.

6. Hold your saw at an angle, and place it in the waste section of a socket right up against the blue painter's tape. Slowly saw at roughly 45 degrees, checking to make sure you are following the blue painter's tape on the endgrain as well as the perpendicular pencil line. Keep sawing until your saw is just touching your marking gauge lines on both the endgrain and face of the socket board. Repeat for all socket walls.

7. Affix a clamp to the edges of the socket board, and grab a card scraper that's about the same thickness as your saw plate. Place the card scraper into the saw kerfs you just created, and use a hammer to pound it directly into the joint. The point of this action is to bring the angled cut you just made with your saw all the way down to the baseline over the entire span of the socket. This makes subsequent waste removal much easier.

8. Remove the socket board from the vise and clamp it firmly on your bench. Remove the waste with a chisel, starting by making a downward chisel chop about ⅛" (3.2mm) from the baseline. Reorient your chisel, so it sticks in the endgrain of the waste section. Using light pressure or mallet taps, remove a small amount of waste.

Removing Socket Board Waste

Compared to through dovetails, where a fret or coping saw does most of the work, removing the waste from your socket board can seem like a slog. If you have a drill press, you can speed up the process. Choose an appropriately sized drill bit and set the stop of your drill press so that the tip of the bit is just above the baseline on the endgrain of your tail board. Then, drill a series of holes in the waste sections of your socket board close to the baseline on the face. These holes will make the waste pop out easily with a chisel chop to the endgrain

Some people can find it hard to pare right up to the baseline on the endgrain of a socket board. To help, I set a router plane to the correct depth and use it to sneak right up to the line. If you don't have a router plane, make a shim to control your chisel while paring.

9. Keep alternating chops—once in the facegrain away from the baseline, once in the endgrain—until you've removed almost all the waste material. When all that remains is a bit of waste near your baselines, register the chisel directly in your knife lines to take your final chops.

10. Continue removing waste. The sockets can be tricky to remove waste from, so don't be afraid to use whatever tools you have to get rid of bits of waste. Your marking knife can be a really helpful tool here.

11. Finish the joint. Once you've removed all waste that would keep the joint from seating, follow steps 18–21 from the previous section to fit and assemble the joint.

The Box/Finger Joint

There are plenty of machine-assisted joints that are great for boxes. Probably the most common one is the box joint. Similar to a dovetail joint, a box joint (or finger joint depending on the size of the "fingers") takes advantage of ample long-grain wood contact to make a solid glue joint.

Cutting box joints is very specific to the type of jig you either build or purchase, so I won't go over how to generally cut them here. In the Salt Cellar chapter (page 64), however, I'll show you how to make a quick, project-specific box joint jig. This should give you a nice introduction to the joint to determine if you want to explore further and invest in something more versatile for future projects.

A box or finger joint requires the use of a specialized jig.

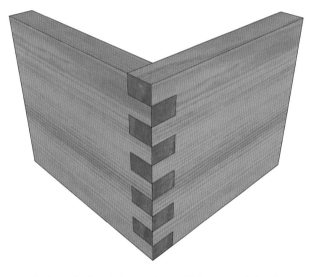

A rendering of a box joint. An incredibly strong joint due to the multiple points of long-grain contact, box joints are easy to execute with a simple jig. They are a great entry into strong wood joinery for the woodworker who prefers power tools.

Additional Joints

While the joints we've discussed are probably the most common and helpful joints you'll encounter when making decorative and practical boxes, there are almost an infinite number of options at your disposal.

There are even specialty router bits that can cut solid joinery right on the router table without the need for additional jigs or fixtures. A lock miter bit allows you to cut a miter joint at the router table, and the geometry of the joint makes it a heck of a lot stronger than a standard miter. And of course, if you are ultimately too intimidated to cut dovetail joints by hand, you can always go with one of the many router dovetail jigs on the market—they'll work just fine in most box-making circumstances.

This list is by no means exhaustive—just know that you don't need to be limited by what I've presented in this chapter. If you're trying to make a box and none of the joints you can think of are working, chances are there's an option out there that will be just perfect for your project and skill level.

Projects

Simple Pine Keepsake Box with Lift Lid

This butt joint box is a great introduction to making wooden boxes. Perfect for storing small items like jewelry or keepsakes, this project not only teaches fundamental woodworking skills but also results in a practical, attractive storage solution. It doesn't require you to learn any challenging or fancy joints, you don't need to rout any grooves, and it can be done with just a few simple tools.

It's also a nice way to get comfortable using hand tools to really dial things in and even do some shaping. We'll go over using a plane to fine tune surfaces in detail—a great skill to have that you'll use repeatedly when making boxes. We'll also use a makeshift rasp to carve out a finger lift that's both attractive and useful.

While this box is intended to be as simple as possible to get you started quickly, there is something to note. The bottom of this box is glued on instead of floating in a groove. Usually this is a big no-no because of wood movement, but because of the size of the box and the stability of the wood chosen, this is completely fine. Just make sure you follow the same principles if you deviate from the plans—don't make the box too wide, and make sure your bottom is made of a relatively stable material.

Tools
- Combination square
- Block plane
- Drill
- Awl
- Clamps
- Flush cut saw
- Pencil
- Vise
- Mallet
- Shooting board
- ¼" (6mm) drill bit
- Compass

Materials:
- White pine, ⅜" (9.5mm) thick, ⅝" (1.6cm) thick, ¼" (6.4mm) thick, and ⅛" (3.2mm) thick
- ¼" (6.4mm) oak dowels
- ½" (1.3cm) oak dowel
- Wood glue
- CA glue
- Finish
- Sandpaper

This project features pinned butt joints and employs a straightforward lift lid. Plans can be found on page 138.

Material	Part	Quantity	Dimensions	Notes
CUT LIST				
White Pine	Sides	2	⅜" x 3" x 10" (9.5mm x 7.6 x 25.4cm)	
White Pine	Ends	2	⅝" x 3" x 3" (1.6 x 7.6 x 7.6cm)	
Pine	Main Top/Bottom	2	¼" x 3⅞" x 10⅛" (6.4mm x 9.8 x 25.7cm)	Intentionally oversized
Pine	Top Inset	1	⅛" x 3⅛" x 8⅞" (3.2mm x 7.9 x 22.5cm)	Intentionally oversized
Nominal Finished Size: 3½" x 3¾" x 10" (8.9 x 9.5 x 25.4cm)				

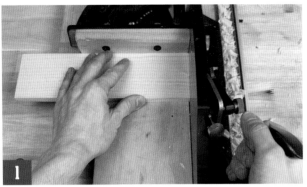

1. Cut all the parts out according to the provided cut list. Then, gather all materials and ensure that all stock is flat and square. One of the most important things about making boxes is that opposing sides must be exactly the same length. This is a good time to get comfortable using the shooting board covered in the Tools chapter (page 13). Use it to dial in opposing sides.

2. Using the plans at the back of the book, mark the location of the dowels on the long box sides with a pencil and awl. It's fine to deviate here a bit, adding or removing a dowel where you see fit. Just make sure that you are always drilling into the center of the box side.

3. Spread a bead of wood glue along the endgrain of the short box sides. Butt them up against the ends of the long box sides and clamp the box together. Spend time making sure that everything here is aligned, using your fingers to feel for any proud wood at the joints. Let the joint sit for about 30 minutes so the glue has time to set.

4. Remove the clamps. The glue joint should be strong enough to withstand installing the dowels. Using a ¼" (6mm) drill bit, drill 1" (2.5cm) deep into the marks you made in Step 1. Drill as straight as possible. Putting a combination square on your workpiece as a visual reference can help, or use a drill press if you have one.

5. Coat ¼" (6.4mm) dowels in wood glue and pound them into the holes. After about 30 minutes, trim the dowels with a flush cut saw, and clean up the joint surface with a hand plane or some sandpaper affixed to a sanding block.

6. Clamp the box in your vise with an end facing up. Using very light cuts with a block plane, level the butt joint on the short sides of the box. Here, we are just trying to fix any mismatch that occurred during glue-up. Try to avoid having your cuts go all the way through to the opposite side. Lift the plane just before it reaches the end. This will help prevent blowout on the endgrain of the opposite side.

7. Before fitting the bottom and top, clean up the edges. Slight misalignments and squeeze-out from glue-up can keep things from coming together properly. Use a pencil to make markings all over the top and bottom edges of the box. Affix some 150-grit sandpaper to your work bench and, using circular motions, sand the top and bottom edges of the box until all the pencil markings are gone.

8. Spread a bead of glue along the bottom edge of the box. Try to keep glue toward the outside on the edge. This will prevent squeeze-out from going inside the box. Press the box bottom onto the edge, square it with the box body, and clamp. The oversized bottom should be proud just a bit on all four box sides.

9. After the glue has dried, trim the box bottom flush with the box sides. Take the top inset and see if it fits inside the box. It will likely be too large. Using a plane and shooting board, trim the lid inset until it just drops inside the box. A little play here is desirable, so make sure the inset isn't too tight.

Flush Trimming with a Block Plane

There are multiple points in this project where you'll need to use a block plane to trim components to final size. This is a helpful skill to pick up. By oversizing parts and trimming them later, you remove the stress of having to get things exactly right with your initial cuts. I use this all the time in box-making, and there are some helpful tips to make the process go smoothly.

Whenever flush trimming, it's always a good idea to

An example of endgrain blowout.

start with the endgrain. This is because if there is any blowout on the exit of the cut, it will likely be planed away when the long grain is flush trimmed.

To avoid blowout completely, skew the plane and only take cuts toward the center of the edge you are trimming, ending your cut before reaching the opposite end. As you plane, rest the sole of the plane against the surface you are flush trimming to—in this case, the side of the box.

Continually check your progress with your fingertips. Once you are close to finishing, retract the blade in your block plane so that it takes a very fine shaving. Continue planing until the surfaces are flush. Once you are finished with the endgrain, flush trim the long grain surfaces, again keeping the sole of the plane resting on the box side as a reference.

Flush planing endgrain.

Flush planing long grain.

10. Using a combination square, make a pencil mark **¹¹⁄₁₆" (1.8cm) from one of the ends and ⁷⁄₁₆" (1.1cm) from the one of the edges of the main top.** Spread wood glue on one side of the top inset, leaving small spots here and there bare for CA glue. Put small dabs of CA glue on the bare spots. These will act as a "clamp" for the inset while the wood glue dries.

11. Carefully line up one of the corners of the inset with the marks you made in the previous step. Once you have things aligned, put downward pressure on the top inset until the CA glue has fully set—about 30 seconds.

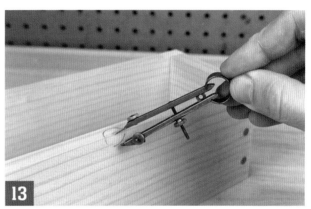

12. Test fit the lid. Just like the bottom, it should be oversized at this point. Trim the lid the same way you trimmed the bottom, making sure the edges of the lid are flush with the sides of the box. Using a block plane, plane a light chamfer to your taste on the edges of the box lid and bottom.

13. Using a compass, mark a ¼" (6.4mm) radius half circle on edges of the box lid. Refer to the plans in the back of the book for detailed drawings and dimensions. Take a ½" (1.3cm) dowel and use double-sided tape to attach some 80- to 150-grit sandpaper to it. With the dowel angled at 45 degrees, sand the edge of the box until you meet your pencil lines. Take your time here. You want to make sure you end up with a nice, even, round finger lift.

14. Surface and sand the box and lid. Then, apply the finish of your choice!

Cherry Keepsake Box

As I mentioned earlier in the joints chapter (see page 16), rabbets are a great way to quickly put together a sturdy drawer without going through the hassle of cutting dovetails. But they also make for attractive standalone boxes, and this box is a great way to get comfortable with the form. This box is great for storing keepsakes, such as photographs, letters, or small collectibles. It's also good storage for everyday items you don't want cluttering up your space.

In this project, we'll introduce the use of a router in box building. Routers can be intimidating, but they are extremely versatile tools. With just a few common bits, you'll be able to cut all the joinery extremely quickly. Another key element of this chapter is the box lid. In just a few simple steps, we'll create a lid that functions as if it is hinged, without the need for expensive and difficult to install hinges.

Along the way, I'll show you some ways to add decorative elements to the box. The pins, lid lift, and fabric-lined bottom all provide you with opportunities to add your own artistic flair to the project. My hope is you'll take all these individual elements and apply them to your own designs as you get more and more comfortable with box building.

The lid of this box is fairly wide and solid wood, so there are some concerns about wood movement (twisting, cupping, etc.). However, as long as you choose a relatively stable wood that has acclimated to its environment, you shouldn't be overly worried.

This project features a pinned and rabbeted joint. Plans can be found on page 139.

Tools

- Router table
- Router
- Combination square
- Block plane
- Drill
- Clamps
- Flush cut saw
- Shooting board
- Trim router
- Band saw
- Rasps
- Files
- Marking knife
- Pencil
- Chisel
- Handsaw
- ⅛" (3mm) upcut spiral router bit
- ¼" (6mm) upcut spiral or straight flute cutter router bit
- ½" (13mm) upcut spiral or straight flute cutter router bit
- ³⁄₁₆" (5mm) brad point drill bit

Materials

- Cherry, ¼" (6mm) thick, ⅜" (1cm) thick, ½" (1.3cm) thick
- Ebony, ³⁄₁₆" (4.8mm) thick
- ³⁄₁₆" (4.8mm) ebony dowels
- Baltic Birch plywood, ¼" (6.4mm) thick
- Wood glue
- Spray adhesive
- Finish
- Sandpaper
- Shellac
- Double-sided tape
- Cotton fabric

CUT LIST				
Material	**Part**	**Quantity**	**Dimensions**	**Notes**
Cherry	Sides	2	½" x 2½" x 12" (1.3 x 6.4 x 30.5cm)	
Cherry	Sides	2	¼" x 2½" x 5½" (6.4mm x 6.4 x 14cm)	
Cherry	Liners	2	¼" x 1⅞" x 4⅞" (6.4mm x 4.8 x 12.4cm)	Intentionally oversized
Cherry	Lid	1	⅜" x 5⅜" x 11½" (9.5mm x 13.7 x 29.2cm)	Intentionally oversized
Ebony	Lid Lift	1	³⁄₁₆" x ⅝" x 2⅛" (4.8mm x 1.6 x 5.4cm)	Intentionally oversized
Baltic Birch Plywood	Bottom	1	¼" x 5⅛" x 11⅞" (6.4mm x 13 x 30.2cm)	
Ebony	Dowels	12	¼" x 1½" (6.4mm x 3.8cm)	

1. Cut all the parts out according to the provided cut list.
Then, gather all materials and ensure that all stock is flat, square, and opposing sides are the exact same length. Using the plans at the back of the book, mark the location of all rabbets using a marking gauge (note that all rabbets are not the same depth and width). Make sure to mark all edges, including the endgrain. This will simplify setup at the router table and help prevent blowout.

2. Chuck a ½" (13mm) upcut spiral or straight flute cutter bit in your router. Then, set the router table fence so that the cutter aligns with your marking gauge line on the ends of the long box sides. Take light passes, pushing your stock with a scrap block to avoid blowout, raising the router bit by about ¹⁄₁₆"- ⅛" (1.6–3.2mm) each time until you reach your final depth.

3. Using the same router bit and fence setting, rout the rabbet along the top edge of the front long box piece. To rout the rabbet along the top edge of the rear long box piece (which is wider than the rabbet on the front long piece), reset the fence and use the same router bit. Again, rout in light passes until you reach final depth.

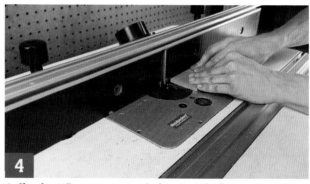

4. Chuck a ¼" (6mm) upcut spiral or straight flute cutter bit in your router. Then, set the router table fence to cut the groove for the box bottom. In light passes, rout the groove along the bottom edge of all four box sides. Note that the groove is significantly deeper on the long box sides. Make sure you don't rout a groove too deep in your short sides or you risk ruining your stock.

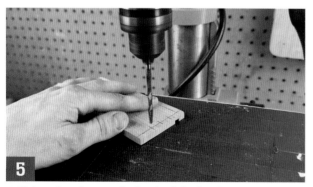

5. Using the plans at the back of the book, mark the location of the dowels on the short box sides with a pencil and awl. Using a ³⁄₁₆" (5mm) brad point drill bit, drill the pin holes in the marked locations. Using a drill press is helpful to stay square, but a hand drill will work just fine.

6. Spray adhesive on one side of the plywood box bottom and the underside of the cotton fabric. Wait about 30 seconds for the adhesive to get tacky, then press the box bottom onto the underside of the fabric. Apply firm pressure, and trim the fabric to the lid using a razor blade.

Tips for a Fabric-Lined Bottom

Fabric is a great way to dress up an otherwise plain and boring plywood box bottom. It's simple, cheap, and you have essentially limitless options at your fingertips.

I always use Baltic birch for plywood box bottoms simply because it is much higher quality than the plywood available at big box stores. Another nice thing about Baltic birch is that it typically comes in standard thicknesses, unlike big box plywood which is slightly thinner than the stated dimensions. This advantage, however, can cause problems when lining with fabric. For example, in this project, I rout a ¼" (6.4mm) groove to fit a ¼" (6.4mm) Baltic birch plywood bottom. Depending on the thickness of the fabric you adhere to the plywood, it may no longer fit into the corresponding groove. While this may seem like a big problem, it's easily overcome. After applying your fabric, test fit it in the groove. If it's too tight, simply rout a shallow rabbet on the underside perimeter of the box bottom until it freely fits into the groove.

Another problem with fabric-lined bottoms is the edges can fray up as you slide your box bottom in—a total disaster! This can be partially overcome by making sure the groove isn't too tight, but for additional insurance, I will apply a coat of shellac over the fabric, paying special attention to the edges. The shellac helps keep any frayed fibers at the edges from straying and causing problems during assembly.

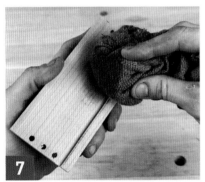

7. Apply a washcoat of shellac to the interior box parts. This will help with glue cleanup later. Spread a bead of glue along the rabbets of the same end of two long pieces and clamp a short piece in place. Slide the box bottom into the groove, spread glue into the other end rabbets on the long pieces, and clamp the remaining short piece in place. I like to apply ample clamping pressure in both directions to ensure everything is nice and snug.

8. After the glue has set for about 30 minutes, remove all clamps. Using the holes you drilled into the short box sides as a guide, drill about 1" (2.5cm) deep into the endgrain of the long box sides. Spread glue on ³⁄₁₆" (4.8mm) dowels and pound them into the holes. Trim the dowels with a flush cut saw, and clean everything up with a hand plane (for more discussion on this process, see page 39).

Choosing Dowels

The pins—or dowels—used in this box are a very prominent feature in the design. Accordingly, when building your own box, you'll want to consider which species of wood to use.

Big box stores typically only have dowels in two species: oak and poplar. While these are perfectly fine structurally, they don't offer too much variety in terms of aesthetics. Specialty woodworking stores generally have dowels in a wider variety of species, but if you really want to be able to use whatever you want, consider purchasing a dowel plate.

A dowel plate is a fairly simple tool. It's just a piece of steel with different sized holes cut in it. You start by preparing some square stock that's just a bit larger than the dowel size you are going for, and then hammer it through the appropriate hole. I prefer a dowel plate with a lot of holes, as you can start with a larger blank and progressively reduce it in size to your final dimension without having to take off too much at once.

A dowel plate will allow you to make dowels out of any type of wood.

9. Using a hand plane and a shooting board, trim the length of the box liners until they just fit into their final locations. Repeatedly check the fit of the liners as you trim them instead of relying on set dimensions. This will ensure that everything fits perfectly.

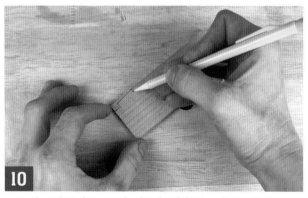

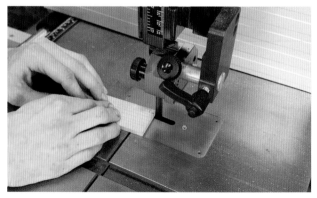

10. Using the plans at the back of the book, mark the slope and notch cuts for the box liners. These cuts are what allow the lid to move freely, so take your time making sure the markings are accurate. Remove the waste however you are most comfortable. I find the band saw to be the easiest method.

11. Clean up the cuts you made in the previous step with sandpaper, files, or rasps. Insert the liners into their final location in the box, and check to make sure the notch at the rear is in line with the rabbet on the rear long box piece. Spread glue on the back side of the liners and clamp them to the short box sides.

12. After the glue has set for about 30 minutes, remove the clamps. If you followed the cut list, your box lid should be too wide and too long to fit into the rabbet along the top edge of the box. Using a shooting board and a hand plane, slowly trim the box top until it just fits into the rabbet. Also test the action of the lid. You want it to be able to open and close freely without sticking.

13. Use a marking knife and combination square to mark the outline of the lid lift on the underside front edge of the box lid. Make a mark 5⁄16" (7.9mm) long, 4½" (11.4cm) from each edge, and then connect the marks. I also like to darken my marking knife lines with a pencil to make sure I can clearly see them for the next step.

14. Using a ⅛" (3mm) upcut spiral bit in a trim router, rout the mortise for the lid lift. Make shallow passes, and stay about 1⁄16" (1.6mm) away from your marking gauge lines. Continue routing until your final depth is just a tad under 3⁄16" (4.8mm).

15. Finish the edges of the mortise by placing an appropriate-sized chisel directly into your marking gauge line. Then, begin chopping along the line. Make sure to chop the sections that run across the grain first, otherwise you risk splitting wood fibers when chopping the section along the grain.

16. Using a shooting board and a hand plane, trim the lid lift until it just fits into the mortise. Spread a bead of glue into the mortise, and clamp the lid lift in place. After the glue has dried, the lid lift will sit a bit proud of the box lid. Plane it flush using a block plane and the techniques covered in the Simple Keepsake Box with Lift Lid project (page 34).

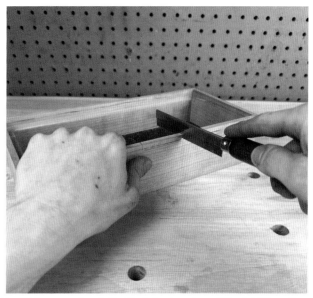

17. Place the lid on the box. At this point, the lid lift will prevent the lid from seating fully. Mark the location of the lid lift on the top edge of the front of the box. Transfer the line to the front using a combination square. Using a handsaw, slowly saw the edge of the box until it meets the depth of the rabbet.

18. Use a clamp or double-sided tape to attach a large block of scrap wood to the front of the box, so it is flush with the top edge. Take your time to make sure everything is lined up and secure here. This scrap will provide your router with a larger bearing surface to make the next step much easier and safer.

19. Using a ⅛" (3mm) upcut spiral bit in a trim router, rout out the notch for the lid lift in the front edge of the box. Stop about ¹⁄₁₆" (1.6mm) from your saw cuts. Continue routing in light passes until you reach the depth of the rabbet. Clean up the ends of the notch with a chisel, and you're done! Finish the exterior of the box with a finish of your choice.

Bubinga Gift Box with Framed Lid

The miter joint is extremely popular among box makers, and for good reason. When executed properly, mitered boxes can look very clean and elegant. And once you get the general process down, it's very easy to batch out a good number of mitered boxes at a time for gifts or to sell at craft fairs. This box, while simple in appearance, has several small design features that bring it all together. The mitered joints make it appear as though the straight grain of the box sides wrap around the corners. Further, since the top and bottom portions of the box are made at the same time and separated later with the band saw, we ensure that the color and grain of the top and bottom match. This versatility makes it ideal for housing anything from collectibles to personal mementos, ensuring both aesthetic appeal and functionality.

This project relies heavily on the mitered shooting board covered earlier in the book, so it's a good idea to make sure you have that built and fully set up. We'll use it to not only cut the miters for the joinery of the box, but also to dial in a perfect friction fit for the interior mitered liner that keeps the lid on. Mitered liners can be used in all kinds of boxes, so you may want to check out that portion of this project even if you don't intend to build it.

One of the best things about box-making is the ability to continually return to a form and make slight variations—in dimension, wood choice, etc.—to change the feel of the final piece. The simplicity of this box makes it a perfect canvas for experimentation. You should feel free to change things up as you see fit.

Tools	
• Combination square	• Router table
• Smoothing plane	• ⅛" (3mm) upcut spiral
• Block plane	or straight flute cutter
• Band clamps	router bit
• Band saw	• Razor blade
• Mitered	• Pencil
shooting board	• Chisel
• Router	• Orbital sander

Materials
- Bubinga, ¼" (6.4mm) thick
- Sitka spruce, ³⁄₁₆" (4.8mm) thick
- Baltic birch plywood, ⅛" (3.2mm) thick
- Decorative paper
- Wood glue
- Painter's tape
- Spray adhesive
- Finish
- Sandpaper
- Shellac
- Double-sided tape

This project features a simple mitered joint. Plans can be found on page 140.

CUT LIST				
Material	Part	Quantity	Dimensions	Notes
Bubinga	Sides	2	¼" x 2⅞" x 7" (6.4mm x 7.3 x 17.8cm)	
Bubinga	Sides	2	¼" x 2⅞" x 3" (6.4mm x 7.3 x 7.6cm)	
Sitka Spruce	Liner	2	³⁄₁₆" x 2⅛" x 6¾" (4.8mm x 5.4 x 17.2cm)	Intentionally oversized
Sitka Spruce	Liner	2	³⁄₁₆" x 2⅛" x 3" (4.8mm x 5.4 x 7.6cm)	Intentionally oversized
Baltic Birch	Top and Bottom	2	⅛" x 3" x 6¾" (3.2mm x 7.6 x 17.2cm)	

Nominal Finished Size: 3¼" x 2¾" x 7" (8.3 x 7 x 17.8cm)

1. Cut all the parts out according to the provided cut list. Then, gather the four main box sides and mark which sides will be the inside faces. Place a piece show-side down on your mitered shooting board with the inside face facing up. Place a hand plane on the 45-degree ramp and begin planing the ends of the box side. Make light passes with the hand plane, making sure you are applying downward pressure against the 45-degree ramp.

2. Continue checking the edge as you plane until you have created a full 45-degree cut. Repeat on both ends of all four box sides. If you cut too much, don't panic—the only thing that really matters here is that opposing sides are the exact same length. Check opposing side lengths against each other, and make light plane passes where appropriate until they are equal.

3. Chuck a ⅛" (3mm) upcut spiral or straight flute cutter bit in your router. Then, set the router table fence so that the cutter is set ⅛" (3.2mm) from the edge of a box side. Rout grooves on both the top and bottom edges of all four main box sides. Remember to take light passes, raising the router bit slightly until you reach final depth.

4. Gather both plywood pieces (see cut list). Spray adhesive on one side of each piece and the underside of some decorative paper of your choice. Wait about 30 seconds for the adhesive to get tacky, then press the plywood pieces onto the underside of the paper. Apply firm pressure and the paper to the plywood using a razor blade. Repeat for the other side of the plywood.

5. Apply a washcoat of shellac to the interior box parts. This will help with glue cleanup later. Place all four box sides with the inside faces down and edges touching. It also helps to set up a straightedge to press the boards against and keep things in alignment. Stretch painter's tape across the joints, pulling tightly before you press down. You want the tape to have a bit of stretch to it as you close the joint.

Lining Plywood with Paper

Just like fabric, decorative papers are a great way to add some flair to the plywood used in boxes. I often find myself perusing the aisles of my local craft store, eyeing any papers that may be useful in future projects.

I've found that the best kind of papers to use are generally heavier than standard printer paper, but thinner than heavy cardstock. Go too thin, and you risk having the adhesive bleed through. Go too thick, and you'll alter the dimensions of the plywood too much, and it might be too snug to fit into its corresponding groove. Another benefit of thicker paper is that you can safely apply a layer of shellac over it to give some extra protection. Paper alone probably won't stand up to the test of time.

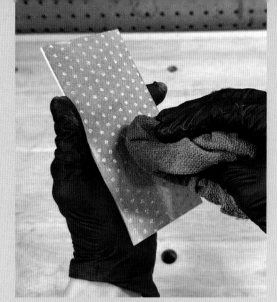

A coat of shellac to decorative paper will help longevity.

Be sure to pair match your box's color scheme when selecting decorative paper.

When choosing papers, remember that your box has both an inside and an outside, and that the colors may vary greatly. In this box, the exterior of the bubinga is much darker than the Sitka spruce interior. When choosing my papers to line the top and bottom, I made sure to match these color schemes. A dark paper for the bright spruce interior would look a bit off compared to the bright and vibrant pattern I chose.

6. Carefully turn all four sides over and lightly brush a 50-50 mixture of wood glue and water on all the miters. Allow it to dry for about 10–30 minutes. This "glue size" will help seal the endgrain and ensure that the ensuing glue joint is much stronger.

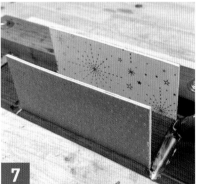
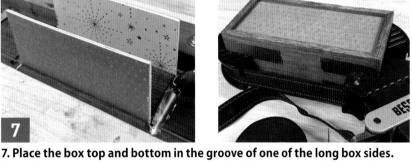

7. Place the box top and bottom in the groove of one of the long box sides. Spread some wood glue on all the miters and fold the joints together carefully, making sure that the top and bottom fit into the grooves on the box sides. If the tape is tight enough, you should feel the joints "snap" together as you bend them. Once all four corners are together, apply tape to the final joint and seal things up. Sometimes, I'll also add a band clamp to keep things nice and tight, although it isn't necessary if your miters are perfect.

8. Allow the glue to set for a minimum of 30 minutes. Then, set a combination square to $^{11}/_{16}$" (1.8cm), and use it to strike a pencil line on one of the short box sides. At the band saw, after ensuring both your blade and fence are square to the table, set the fence so that the blade aligns with the pencil line you just drew.

9. Carefully saw the box lid from the box body. As you push the box through the band saw blade, you'll feel differences in resistance depending on where the cut is. Make sure you are attentive. Keep your feed rate as steady as possible, and always use a push block. At the end of the cut, you should have completely separated the box top from the bottom.

10. Affix some 150-grit sandpaper to your workbench. Using circular motions, sand the top and bottom edges of both the box and the lid until all band saw marks are gone. Repeatedly place the lid on top of the box, checking where they meet for any gaps. Once both edges are truly ready and flat, the lid and box should be indistinguishable where they meet. *Note: Keep the sandpaper affixed to your bench. We'll be using it later to surface the box and liner.*

11. Clean up any glue squeeze-out on the interior of the box. Any remaining glue in the corners could cause problems when fitting the liner, so spend your time cleaning things up with an old chisel. Don't worry about leaving any surface imperfections on the interior; it's going to be completely covered by the liner.

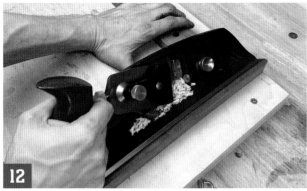

12. Gather the four liner pieces and fully sand the inside faces. Place a long liner piece show side up on your mitered shooting board with the inside face facing up. Place a hand plane on the 45-degree ramp, and begin planing the ends of the liner side. Make light passes with the hand plane, making sure you are applying downward pressure against the 45-degree ramp.

13. Check the liner sides. In the cut list, the liner sides are left intentionally long. This is because instead of relying on absolute dimensions, it's better to just plane the liner pieces to size. After you've established full 45-degree miters on both ends of the liner piece, check to see if it fits inside the box. If it doesn't (and it shouldn't at first), plane to size on the mitered shooting board until it just slides in the box. It's good to check often as you plane. The worst thing in the world is ending up with a liner piece that is too short!

14. After you've fit the first long liner piece, repeat the same process for both short liner pieces and insert them in the box. The last liner piece is the hardest one to get in. Make sure it is nice and snug, but not so tight that you can't seat it fully. Once the final piece is in, the friction fit should be enough to keep the liner from ever coming out.

15. With the liner fit, you can now put the box together and have the lid stay on. With the box assembled, return to the sandpaper affixed to your bench and surface the sides, moving gently back and forth along the grain. Finishing your box sides like this will prevent you from rounding over the corners with an unwieldy orbital sander and leave everything nice and crisp. Use some sandpaper to break the outside edges of the box and apply the finish of your choice!

Refining the Liner

After you've fit the liner, you might find that things aren't working out perfectly—namely, the lid might be simply too tight to fit. Luckily, there are some simple steps to get everything working just right.

Use double-sided tape to affix some sandpaper to one side of a square scrap of wood. Make sure you trim the sandpaper, so it doesn't roll around the edges. Place the block on the edge of the box, and lightly sand the outside edge of the liner. Do this to all four sides of the liner, continually checking the fit of the lid. After just a bit of sanding, you should end up with a lid that fits perfectly.

You also may find that the top edges of your liner pieces aren't on the same plane. This is easily fixed with some sandpaper on your bench. Just repeat the process outlined in step 10 until everything is lined up.

To top things off, use the sanding block you made to apply a light chamfer to the outside edge of the liner. This will help the lid slide into place more easily than leaving things square.

Curly Maple Trinket Box with Ebony Pull

The purpose of the previous project was to get you comfortable with executing miters in boxes—a skill you'll frequently utilize if you plan on making a career in box-making. Now that you've honed your skills in crafting precise joints, let's enhance your projects with some decorative flair that you can apply across any future endeavors.

For this box, we delve into using veneer strips to craft an eye-catching checkerboard bottom, an element that elevates its visual appeal, making it perfect for storing cherished collectibles or storing valuable keepsakes. The simple tools required—a hand plane, some blue painter's tape, and a bit of wood glue—make this addition not only accessible but also a delightful challenge.

Following the veneer work, we'll transition to the lathe to craft a custom pull for the lid, utilizing an open-ended wrench to ensure perfect sizing of the pull's tenon, Opt for tightly straight-grained veneer to maintain clarity in the checkerboard pattern, and source your material for the pull from pen turning blanks available at woodworking stores, allowing you to select from a variety of species without significant expense.

Tools
- Combination square
- Smoothing plane
- Block plane
- Lathe and turning chisels (roughing gouge, parting tool, spindle gouge)
- Chisels
- Band clamps
- ¼" (6mm) open-ended wrench
- Router
- Router table
- ¼" (3mm) upcut spiral and straight flute cutter router bit
- Mitered shooting board
- Table saw
- Razor blade
- Drill
- ¼" (6mm) brad point drill bit
- 2" (51mm) Forstner bit
- Ruler
- Pencil
- Fine cut saw or dovetail saw
- Vise
- Flush cut saw

Materials
- Curly maple, ¼" (6.4mm) thick
- Curly maple, ⁵⁄₁₆" (7.9mm) thick
- Ebony turning blank, ¾" (1.9cm) square
- Leopardwood veneer, ¹⁄₁₆" (1.6mm) thick
- Baltic birch plywood, ⅛" (3.2mm) thick
- Wood glue
- Painter's tape
- Bronze metallic paint
- Finish
- Sandpaper
- Paste wax
- Shellac

This box utilizes mitered joints and features a lathe-turned pull. Plans can be found on page 141.

Material	Part	Quantity	Dimensions	Notes
CUT LIST				
Curly Maple	Sides	2	¼" x 2⅝" x 4" (6.4mm x 6.7 x 10.2cm)	
Curly Maple	Top	1	⁵⁄₁₆" x 3⅞" x 3⅞" (7.9mm x 9.8 x 9.8cm)	Intentionally oversized
Baltic Birch	Bottom	1	⅛" x 3¾" x 3¾" (3.2mm x 9.5 x 9.5cm)	
Ebony	Turning Blank	1	¾" x ¾" x 6" (1.9 x 1.9 x 15.2cm)	
Leopardwood	Veneer Strips	6	¹⁄₁₆" x ¾" x 6" (1.6mm x 1.9 x 15.2cm)	

Nominal Finished Size: 2⅝" x 4" x 4" (6.7 x 10.2 x 10.2cm)

1. Cut all the parts out according to the provided cut list. Then, gather the four main box sides and mark which sides will be the inside faces. Place a piece show-side down on your mitered shooting board with the inside face facing up. Place a hand plane on the 45-degree ramp, and begin planing the ends of the box side. Make light passes with the hand plane, making sure you are applying downward pressure against the 45-degree ramp. Continue checking the edge as you plane until you have created a full 45-degree cut. Repeat on both ends of all four box sides until opposing sides are equal.

2. Chuck a ¼" (6mm) upcut spiral or straight flute cutter bit in your router. Then, set the router table fence so that the cutter is set ⅛" (3.2cm) from the edge of a box side. Rout grooves on only the bottom edges of all four box sides. Remember to make light passes, raising the router bit slightly until you reach final depth.

3. Adjust the router table fence to cut the rabbet on the top edge of the box sides. This requires embedding the bit in the router fence so only ⅛" (3.2cm) of the cutter engages your stock . Rout the rabbet on only the top edges of all four box sides.

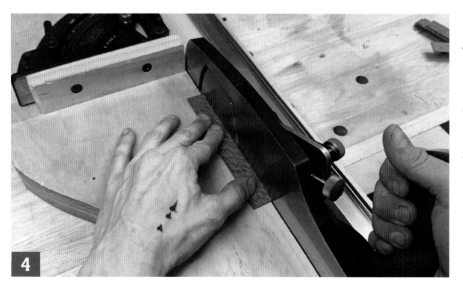

4. Gather the veneer strips listed in the cut list. They should be ripped into ¾" (1.9cm) strips from a sheet of ¹⁄₁₆" (1.6mm) veneer. Chances are that the edges of your veneer strips won't be perfectly straight after ripping. To fix this, lay a veneer strip down on a 90-degree shooting board and use a hand plane to joint the edge. Make light plane passes until you get a consistent shaving over the entire length of a veneer strip. Do this for both edges of all veneer strips.

5. Take all the veneer strips, stack them, and wrap them together with blue painter's tape. At the table saw, use a scrap piece of veneer to set a stop block on a crosscut sled. This will ensure that when you cut your veneer squares, they are indeed square. Butt the end of your veneer packet against the stop block, and make a series of crosscuts to turn your veneer strips into many packets of veneer squares.

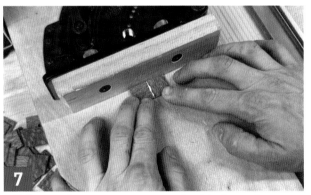

6. Unwrap the packets of veneer squares and gather a small pot of wood glue, blue painter's tape, and a shooting board. Apply an ample coating of paste wax to the surface of your shooting board. This will help prevent the veneer squares from sticking as you assemble the pattern. Dip the edge of one veneer square in wood glue and set it flat on your shooting board.

7. Take another veneer square and, with the grain rotated 90 degrees, press it against the glue-covered edge of the first square. Press the edge of the two glued squares against the shooting board fence, and stretch a small piece of blue painter's tape across the joint. If you pressed down hard, the squares may have lightly adhered to the shooting board. Delicately shift them laterally to release them, or use the edge of a razor blade to carefully pry them off.

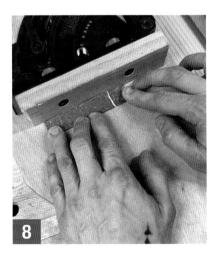

8. Continue the process outlined in steps 6 and 7 to create a row of five veneer squares. Make sure you rotate the grain on each adjacent square. After you have finished a row, you may find it wants to "curl" up due to the tension of the blue painter's tape. To prevent this, tape a completed row flat on a waxed portion of your bench while the glue sets. Continue making veneer rows, taping them to your bench as you work, until you have five completed rows.

9. Joint the edges. After the glue for the rows has dried (about 30 minutes or so), you'll likely have to joint the edges. Place a row on a shooting board, and use a hand plane to joint the edge just like in step 4. Since the grain of adjacent squares is rotated 90 degrees, it's wise to set your plane to make a very light pass here. Repeat this process for both edges of all veneer rows.

10. Spread glue on the edge of one veneer row and place it flat on the shooting board. Take another veneer row and, making sure the grain of each adjacent square is rotated 90 degrees, press it against the glue-covered edge of the first row. Press the edge of the two glued rows against the shooting board fence, and stretch a small piece of blue painter's tape across the joint. Continue this process until all rows have been glued and joined. Flip the square over to view the untaped side and confirm that all squares are properly aligned.

11. Spread an ample amount of wood glue on both sides of the ⅛" (3.2mm)-thick piece of plywood specified in the cut list. Press the veneer pattern firmly on one side and a piece of poplar veneer on the other side. Use your fingers to align both veneer sheets to one corner of the plywood packet and stretch blue painter's tape over the edges. This will help prevent things from shifting when clamped.

12. Line two scrap pieces of plywood or MDF with blue painter's tape and sandwich the veneer packet between them. Clamp the sandwich together and let the glue set for at least 30 minutes. After the glue has fully dried, remove the veneer packet from the clamps and pull off all the blue painter's tape. Joint one edge of the packet on a shooting board, and then use this as a reference edge at the table saw (or stay at the shooting board) to trim the bottom to the dimensions listed in the plans.

13. Apply a washcoat of shellac to the interior box parts. This will help with glue cleanup later. Place all four box sides with the inside faces down and edges touching. It also helps to set up a straight edge to press the boards against and keep things in alignment. Stretch blue painter's tape across the joints, pulling tightly before you press down. You want the tape to have a bit of stretch to it as you close the joint.

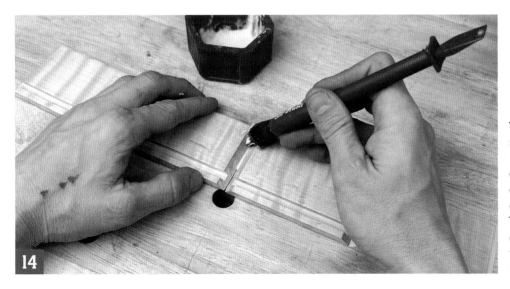

14. Carefully turn all four sides over and lightly brush a 50/ 50 mixture of wood glue and water on all the miters. Allow to dry for about 10–30 minutes. This will help seal the endgrain and ensure that the ensuing glue joint is much stronger.

15. Place the bottom in the groove of one of the box sides. Spread some wood glue on all the miters, and fold the joints together carefully, making sure that the top and bottom fit into the grooves on the box sides. If the tape is tight enough, you should feel the joints "snap" together as you bend them. Once all four corners are together, apply tape to the final joint and seal things up. Sometimes, I'll also add a band clamp to keep things nice and tight, although it isn't necessary if your miters are perfect.

16. After the glue has set, remove all clamps and tape and test fit the box top specified in the cut list. You may find that the top is too tight to fit comfortably in the box's rabbet. Refine the fit with a hand plane at the shooting board until you are satisfied. Mark the center of the top, and at the drill press, use a 2" (51mm) Forstner bit the create a recess ⅛" (3.2mm) deep. Then, using a ¼" (6mm) brad point bit, drill all the way through the center of the top, using a sacrificial scrap underneath to prevent blowout.

17. Mark the center of both ends of the ebony turning blank specified in the cut list and drill a shallow hole with a ¼" (6mm) drill bit. Using the holes you just drilled, mount the blank on the lathe with a spur drive and live center (i.e. "turning between centers" using the accessories that likely came with your lathe instead of using a costly chuck).

18. With the lathe spinning at its highest speed, use a roughing gouge to turn the blank to round. I like to repeatedly check to see if my blank is round by gently resting my gouge on top of the spinning blank. If it's a bumpy ride, then it isn't round yet.

19. With the lathe off, use a ruler to mark the critical locations of the pull with a pencil. Here, you're mainly marking where it begins and ends (you should have a bit of waste at both ends) and where the tenon will be. You can also use this time to mark pencil lines where there are any large changes in the profile of the pull. After you've made the initial markings, turn the lathe on at low speed, and press your pencil against the blank where the markings are to have them transferred around the entire blank.

20. Use a parting tool to define the location of the pull's tenon. The tenon will ultimately be ¼" (6.4mm) in diameter, so try to bring the tenon down to about ⁵⁄₁₆" (7.9mm) at this stage. After you have your tenon well established and oversized, gather a ¼" (6mm) open-ended wrench. With the wrench pressed against the tenon on the backside, use the parting tool carefully with one hand to reduce the size of the tenon until the open end of the wrench just fits over it.

21. Use a spindle gouge to shape the pull to your desired profile. You can use the plans in the back of the book as a guide or use your imagination—as long as the tenon remains the correct size, you won't have problems later.

22. After you've shaped the pull to your liking, sand through the grits with the lathe on. Before I switch grits, I'll turn the lathe off and sand briefly along the grain to remove any cross-grain scratches. Use the parting tool again to carfefully bring the waste sections at both ends of the pull down to about ³⁄₁₆" (4.8mm).

23. Use a fine cut saw or dovetail saw to cut the pull free from the blank. On the bottom of the pull, you don't need to worry about any clean up since it's just a tenon, but at the top, you'll be left with an unsightly nub. There are a lot of complicated ways of removing this, but I find just chipping it away with a chisel and cleaning things up with sandpaper to be wholly sufficient.

24. Back at the box top, paint the indentation that you made with the Forstner bit. I used bronze paint here because the metallic elements give a nice reflection, and the color ties in nicely to the leopwardwood veneer bottom. After the paint has dried, apply a dab of glue inside the ¼" (6.4mm) through hole and press the tenon of the pull through. Wait about 30 minutes for the glue to dry.

25. Flip the top over. I like to do this on my vise with the jaws open enough to allow the pull to pass between them. Then, use a flush cut saw to trim the tenon excess. Surface the box and the box top. Then, use some sandpaper to break all outside edges, and apply the finish of your choice!

Salt Cellar with Finger Joints

This salt cellar is a nice little project that you can finish easily in an afternoon, and one that I guarantee you'll return to repeatedly. It's also our first introduction to true interlocking joinery. Up until this point, we've either relied solely on glue or additional reinforcements when preparing our joints. These interlocking joints are not only attractive, they're also much easier to assemble and provide a great deal of strength compared to those covered in our previous projects. Ideal for holding cooking salts or spices, this sturdy yet elegant box showcases the functional beauty of finger joints, making it a versatile addition to any kitchen or dining setting.

To start, we'll make a very quick-and-dirty box joint jig using an old miter gauge and some scrap plywood. Any box joint jig will work, of course, but if you aren't interested in spending all your time and money making a fancy jig, what we go over here will get the job done just fine. Any router table (or table saw) will also work. Just make sure it has a miter slot that will work with your miter gauge. Just know that all the dimensions—the width of the joints, the size of the cutter, the height of the cutter, etc.—are absolutely critical for the joint to work properly. Further, the order of operations and how you set up your boards to cut the joinery really do matter, so spend your time reading over the steps and practicing on some scrap if you can. As long as you follow all the steps and take your time when making the jig, everything should come together perfectly.

The great thing about this project is that, once you build the jig, you can easily batch out plenty of boxes in an afternoon. That could come in quite handy around the holidays when you're trying to cross names off your list.

This project utilizes a box/finger joint. Plans can be found on page 142.

Tools

- Combination square
- Block plane
- Clamps
- Miter gauge
- Router table
- ¼" (6mm) spiral upcut or straight flute cutter router bit
- Table saw
- Vise
- Pencil
- Shooting board

Materials

- Cherry, ¼" (6.4mm) thick and ³⁄₁₆" (4.8mm) thick
- Plywood, ½" (1.3m) thick
- Wood glue
- CA glue
- Finish
- Sandpaper
- Screws

CUT LIST				
Material	**Part**	**Quantity**	**Dimensions**	**Notes**
Cherry	Sides	2	¼" x 2¼" x 4" (6.4mm x 5.7 x 10.2cm)	
Cherry	Sides	2	¼" x 2¼" x 3" (6.4mm x 5.7 x 7.6cm)	
Cherry	Main Top and Bottom	2	³⁄₁₆" x 3⅛" x 4⅛" (4.8mm x 7.9 x 10.5cm)	Intentionally oversized
Cherry	Top Inset	1	³⁄₁₆" x 2⁹⁄₁₆" x 3⁹⁄₁₆" (4.8mm x 6.5 x 9.1cm)	Intentionally oversized
Scrap Plywood	Scrap Piece	1	½" x 3½" x 12" (1.3 x 8.9 x 30.5cm)	
Square Hardwood	Stock for Jig	2	¼" x ¼" x 3" (6.4 x 6.4mm x 7.6cm)	
Nominal Finished Size: 2⅝" x 3" x 4" (6.7 x 7.6 x 10.2cm)				

1. Start by gathering a miter gauge and the scrap plywood specified in the cut list. Using appropriate-length screws, attach the miter gauge to the leftmost side of the plywood. This assumes that the cutter (in my case, the router bit) is to the right of the miter slot. If yours is to the left, then attach the miter gauge to the rightmost side of the plywood.

2. Chuck a ¼" (6.4mm) straight flute or spiral upcut bit in your router table. Then, raise it exactly ¼" (6.4mm) from the surface of the table. Ensure that the miter gauge is properly set at 90 degrees and insert it into the miter slot. Turn on the router and slowly advance the miter gauge toward the bit, cutting a slot all the way through the plywood fence.

3. Take a piece of the ¼" (6.4mm) square stock from the cut list, and glue it into the slot using a small dab of CA glue. Make sure that this "pin" is projecting out of the front of the plywood fence and not the back.

4. With the router off, reinsert the miter gauge into the miter slot. Unscrew the plywood fence from the miter gauge and shift it over to the left by exactly ¼" (6.4mm). To do this precisely, place another piece of the ¼" (6.4mm) square stock from the cut list directly between the pin in the plywood fence and the router bit. Secure the miter gauge to the plywood fence using a clamp and reattach it with screws. And with that, the jig is all finished!

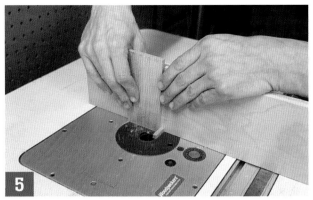 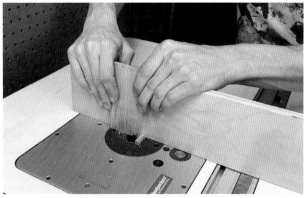

5. Cut all parts out according to the provided cut list. Then, gather the four box sides and ensure they are square. Take one of the long sides, and hold it upright against the plywood fence with the left edge placed firmly on the pin. Hold the piece very tightly against the fence (or better yet, use a clamp), turn the router on, and slowly slide the miter gauge toward the spinning bit until the first cut is complete.

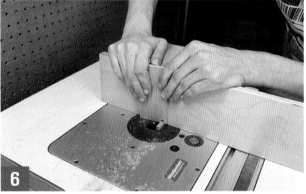 

6. Pull the miter gauge back away from the router bit. On the piece you just cut, there will be a notch at the bottom that is exactly the same size as the pin. Fit this notch over the pin, secure the board tightly against the fence, and make the next cut. Repeat along the edge of the board until you have cut four total notches.

7. Repeat steps 5 and 6. Do this for both ends of the long box sides.

8. To cut the short box sides, start by setting the rightmost notch of a long side over the jig pin and firmly place a short side against it. Hold the piece very tightly against the fence (or use a clamp), turn the router on, and slowly slide the miter gauge toward the spinning bit until the first cut is complete.

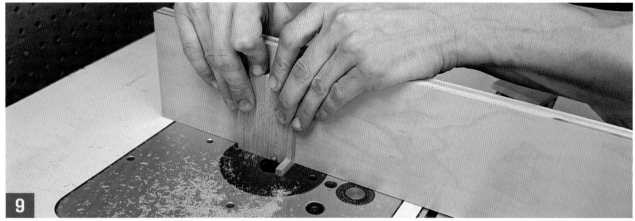

9. Pull the miter gauge back away from the router bit. Slide the piece over against the pin, secure the board tightly against the fence, and make the next cut. Repeat along the edge of the board until you have cut five total notches.

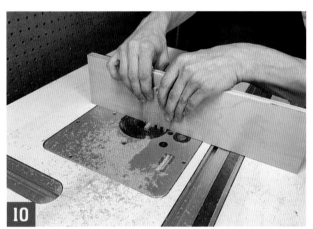

10. Repeat steps 8 and 9 for both ends of the short box sides. Take all four box sides and test the fit. The joints should be nice and snug but not so tight that you can't easily seat everything. If the joint isn't fitting properly, it is likely that something went wrong during the setup of the jig. Check those steps and practice on some scrap until everything is dialed in.

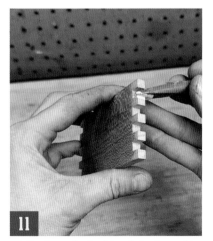

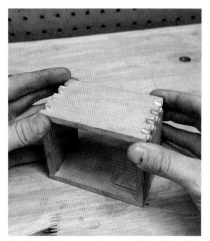

11. Surface the inside of the box sides and finish with a washcoat of shellac. Spread glue on the inside walls of the joints on the long box sides and assemble the box. Make sure that all the joints close up, and apply clamping pressure as needed. You may find that you need clamps in some places and not others for everything to work right. Allow the glue to set for at least 30 minutes.

12. Clamp the box in your vise with an end facing up. Making very light cuts with a block plane, surface the sides of the box to level out the box joints. Try to avoid having your cuts go all the way through to the opposite side. Lift the plane just before it reaches the end. This will help prevent blowout on the endgrain of the opposite side.

13. Before fitting the bottom and top, clean up the edges. Slight misalignments and squeeze out from glue up can keep things from coming together properly. Use a pencil to make markings all over the top and bottom edges of the box. Affix some 150-grit sandpaper to your work bench and, using circular motions, sand the top and bottom edges of the box until all pencil markings are gone.

14. Spread a bead of glue along the bottom edge of the box. Try to keep the glue toward the outside on the edge. This will prevent squeeze out from going inside the box. Press the box bottom onto the edge, square it with the box body, and clamp. The oversized bottom should be proud just a bit on all four box sides.

15. After the glue has dried, trim the box bottom flush with the box sides. Start by trimming the endgrain first. If there is any blowout, you will be able to plane it away when trimming the long grain. For tips on how to properly flush surfaces with a plane, see the sidebar on page 38.

16. Take the top inset piece from the cut list and see if it fits inside the box. It will likely be too large. Using a plane and shooting board, trim the lid inset until it just drops inside the box. A little play here is desirable, so make sure the inset isn't too tight.

17. Using a combination square, make a pencil mark ⁵⁄₁₆" (7.9mm) from one of the ends and ⁵⁄₁₆" (7.9mm) from the one of the edges of the main top. Spread wood glue on one side of the top inset, leaving small spots here and there bare for CA glue. Put small dabs of CA glue on the bare spots. This will act as a "clamp" for the inset while the wood glue dries.

18. Carefully line up one of the corners of the inset with the marks you made in the previous step. Once you have things aligned, put downward pressure on the top inset until the CA glue has fully set—about 30 seconds.

19. Test fit the lid. Just like the bottom, it should be oversized at this point. Trim the lid the same way you trimmed the bottom, making sure the edges of the lid are flush with the sides of the box. Using a block plane, plane a light chamfer to your taste on the edges of the box lid and bottom.

20. Surface and sand box and lid. Then, apply a finish of your choice.

Two-Tone Sliding Lid Dovetail Box

If you plan on making wooden boxes, it's a good idea to get comfortable with dovetails. This project is perfect for getting your feet wet. The design is relatively simple, focusing mainly on cutting joinery, and since there is no hardware or fasteners, most materials can be sourced from your scrap bin.

While this project serves as an introduction to dovetailed boxes, it incorporates advanced concepts like preparing and creating a sliding lid that requires careful planning. These skills will help you craft all types of dovetailed boxes. We'll also introduce some basic carving to add functional and visual interest to the lid—a great woodworking skill to develop.

This versatile form allows for customization inside with dividers and partitions to organize and display personal mementos or keepsakes, making each box uniquely yours. Since the sliding lid is solid wood, opt for rift or quartersawn stock to minimize warping and ensure smooth operation over time. Feel free to experiment and personalize as you see fit!

Tools
- Combination square
- Dovetail saw
- Dividers
- Chisels, ¼"–1" (6–25mm)
- Marking gauge
- Fret or coping saw
- Mallet
- Bevel gauge
- Marking knife
- Block plane
- Jack plane
- Shoulder plane (optional)
- Router table
- F-clamps
- Carving gouges
- Pencil
- ¼" (6mm) straight flute and spiral upcut router bit
- Drill with fine bit
- Table saw
- Band saw
- Miter saw
- #6 15mm sweep carving gouge

Materials
- Cherry, ⁹⁄₁₆" (1.4cm) thick
- Yellow pine, ¼" (6.4mm) thick and ⁹⁄₁₆" (1.4cm) thick
- Wood glue
- Blue painter's tape
- Finish
- Sandpaper
- Masking tape
- Double-sided tape
- Shellac

This box utilizes dovetail joints and features a sliding lid. Plans can be found on page 143.

	CUT LIST			
Material	**Part**	**Quantity**	**Dimensions**	**Notes**
Cherry	Sides	2	⁹⁄₁₆" x 4 ½" x 14" (1.4 x 11.4 x 35.6cm)	
Cherry	Back	1	⁹⁄₁₆" x 4 ½" x 6⅜" (1.4 x 11.4 x 16.2cm)	
Cherry	Front	1	⁹⁄₁₆" x 3⅞" x 6⅜" (1.4 x 9.8 x 16.2cm)	
Pine	Top	1	⁹⁄₁₆" x 5 ¾" x 15" (1.4 x 14.6 x 38.1cm)	(Intentionally oversized)
Pine	Bottom	1	¼" x 5 ¾" x 13³⁄₁₆" (6.4mm x 14.6 x 33.5cm)	

Nominal Finished Size: 4½" x 6⅜" x 14" (11.4 x 16.2 x 35.6cm)

Skill Building

This project will guide you through the following techniques:

- How to cut and fit dovetails
- How to level your box
- How to plan and create a sliding lid
- How to perform basic carving cuts

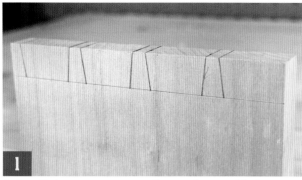

1. Cut all the parts out according to the provided cut list. Then, gather all materials and ensure that all stock is flat and square. Using the plans at the back of the book, mark the location of the dovetails on the tail boards. Pay special attention here. The dovetails at the front of the box are laid out differently than the back.

2. Cut the dovetails as described on pages 22–26. Then, cover the endgrain of the tail boards with blue painter's tape. Take note that the front pin board and the rear pin board have different widths. When transferring the tails on the front pin board, make sure to align the pin and tail boards at the bottom edge, not the top edge.

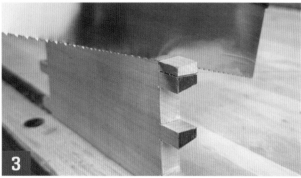

3. Cut the pins as described on pages 27–28. Note that, unlike most dovetail joints, the front pin board has waste at the top edge. Remove this the same way the half-pin at the edge of the tail board is removed, paying attention to angle your saw to match the angle of the pin wall. When all pins are cut, assemble and fit all four box sides.

Leveling a Box

No matter how well you align your boards when transferring your tails, usually you will end up with a little offset where the bottom and top edges of adjoining boards don't meet. Since these edges are referenced against the fence of your router table, this mismatch will be transferred to the grooves when routing. The result will be grooves that do not line up at the corners, preventing both the top and bottom from sliding in properly.

An offset might seem small at first but will lead to big alignment problems.

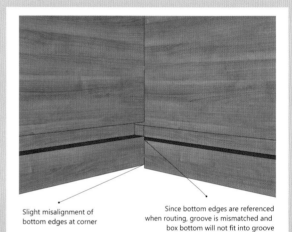

Slight misalignment of bottom edges at corner

Since bottom edges are referenced when routing, groove is mismatched and box bottom will not fit into groove properly

Luckily, this is easy to fix—all you have to do is get rid of this offset. The easiest way I've found is by bringing edges down to the same plane with a block plane. After this, grab a larger plane and slowly plane around the box edge, making sure to keep the plane on at least two edges as you go. Once you get a full shaving all the way around the edge of the box, you're good to go.

Leveling the box edges with a block plane.

4. With the box assembled, level both the box top and bottom. After all edge misalignment has been handled, rest a marking knife against the edge of the box front and make a mark on the box side. This line will be used to locate the groove for the box top. Instead of relying on the dimensions in the plans, using this mark to set the router table ensures it is more precisely located.

5. Take the box apart and transfer the mark you made in the previous step to the endgrain of the tail board. Using the dimensions in the plans, mark the locations for the bottom groove stops on the face of the tail boards. On the endgrain of the tail boards, mark the location of the bottom groove. You only need to do this for one of the tail boards. We'll use it to set up the router table and rout both boards.

6. Chuck a ¼" (6mm) straight flute or spiral upcut bit in your router table. Using the bottom groove location you marked in the previous step, set the router fence. Place some masking tape on the fence in front of the bit. Using a combination square, mark the extremes of the router bit on the masking tape.

7. Take the tail board you marked in Step 5, and place the bottom edge against the router fence. Place the board so the router bit will go past the groove stop line on your tail board just a bit. The geometry of the router bit requires this. Otherwise, the groove will not be long enough. With the board still in place, clamp a stop block to your router table fence against the opposite end of the tail board. Repeat this step for the opposite side of the router table fence using the other end of the tail board.

8. Ensure that your fence and stops are firmly locked. Raise the router bit about ⅛" (3.2mm) from the table and turn the router on. Place the right end of the tail board against the right stop and slowly drop the board onto the spinning router bit. Slowly push the board from right to left until you reach the left stop. Turn off the router, remove the tail board, raise the bit ⅛" (3.2mm), and repeat until you are at full depth on both tail boards. *Important: Make sure you are routing only the bottom groove!*

9. Using the same fence settings, rout the bottom through grooves in both pin boards. (The stops will be well out of the way.) Use a pencil to mark the location of the right stop on your router fence, and remove it. Using a tail board with the marks you made in Step 5, set the router fence location for the top groove.

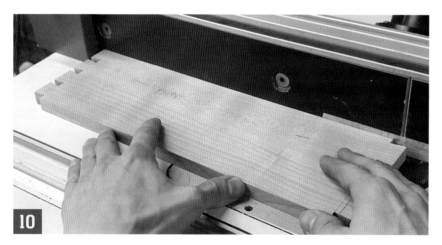

10. Rout the top groove in the first tail board. Note how this groove goes through the half tail at the front and is stopped in the back. This is why only one stop from the previous step is kept on the fence. After you have routed the groove for the first tail board, remove the left stop, replace the right stop where you marked with a pencil in the previous step, and repeat. Using the same fence settings, rout the top groove in the rear pin board only. The front tail board has no top groove.

Preparing for Glue Up

Gluing up a dovetailed box is a very stressful task—there's a lot to juggle while you're up against the clock of the glue setting. But if you take some preparatory steps, the whole process can be a lot less daunting.

The first step before any glue up is a dry fit. Assemble your box by joining the two pin boards to one tail board. Slide the bottom into the groove and join the opposing tail board. Check and see if the bottom is too wide or too long. If it is, the box won't be able to close. Note that, in the plans, the width of the bottom is slightly undersized to allow for expansion and contraction. During the dry fit, ensure that this is still the case.

Now is also a good time to check and make sure the top edge of the box front is aligned with the bottom of the groove for the box top. In the second photo at right, you can see that the edge is slightly above the groove. To correct this, I simply disassembled the box and planed that edge until it met the groove.

With the box disassembled, slide the box bottom into the bottom groove of a pin board. Center the bottom and mark the center of both the bottom and the pin board. When you assemble the box, you can align these marks to ensure that the bottom is centered in the groove. This allows the bottom to expand and contract properly, saving you from a cracked bottom in the future.

If you're worried about getting even clamping pressure, make some clamping cauls. Cut a 1" (2.5cm)-wide piece of scrap to about the width of your tail boards. Place the scrap on the tails and mark the location where the pins will come through. Make notch cuts in these locations with a table saw. Before glue up, use double-sided tape to attach the cauls to your tails. The clamps are placed on the cauls, ensuring even pressure is applied across the width of the joint.

And as I've stated previously in other projects, it's always a good idea to do a wash coat of shellac on the interior of the box before gluing up to make cleaning up any squeeze out much easier.

First, slide the bottom in to ensure fit.

Check to make sure the top edge of the box front aligns with the groove for the box top.

Mark the center of the bottom and sides to make sure the bottom is centered during assembly.

Mark the cut location for clamping cauls.

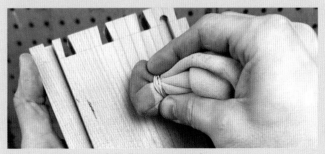
Apply a washcoat of shellac to interior box parts.

11. After preparing for glue up, spread glue on the pin walls of the same side of both pin boards and attach the corresponding tail board. With the pin boards facing up on your bench, spread wood glue in the center inch (2.5cm) or so of the bottom grooves on both pin boards. Do not put glue in any other part of the grooves! This strategic glue placement will keep the floating bottom in place while allowing it to expand and contract.

12. Slide in the box bottom, and center it along the width of the pin boards. See Preparing for Glue Up (page 77) for a helpful tip on this. Spread glue on the remaining exposed pin walls and attach the other tail board. Apply clamps to the tails (or cauls) until the joint fully closes. Check for square by measuring corner to corner. If the distance between the corners isn't the same, skew your clamps slightly and keep checking the corner-to-corner measurement. This can take a bit of trial and error.

13. While the box is drying, gather the board you prepared for the box top. Check its width against the groove in the box to make sure it will fit. You want it to have a slight gap to allow it to slide freely and expand, if necessary. If the lid is too wide, trim it to size at the table saw, band saw, or simply use a hand plane.

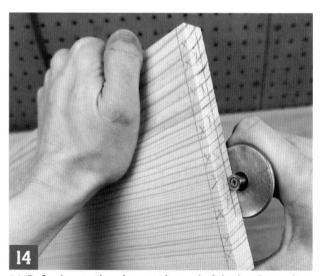

14. Referring to the plans at the end of the book, mark the location for the lid rabbets using a marking gauge. Pay attention to which side you want to be the leading edge of the lid. This side does not get a rabbet. Also, keep in mind that the face you'll be putting your marks on will be the show face of the lid.

15. Using the marks you made, set the router table fence. Taking light passes, rout the rabbet for the lid on all three sides. I like to use a scrap block for the cross-grain cut as it helps control blowout at the exit of the cut. Once you have reached the final depth, check to ensure the lid freely slides in and out of the box groove.

16. With the lid fully seated in the box, mark a pencil line where the bottom of the lid meets the box. Trim the lid to this line on a table or miter saw. I like to then refine the length with a block plane until the lid is completely flush with the box front. Draw a 1¼" (3.2cm) diameter circle 1" (2.5cm) from the center of the leading edge of the lid and, using a fine drill bit, drill a hole ³⁄₁₆" (4.8m) deep into the center of the hole.

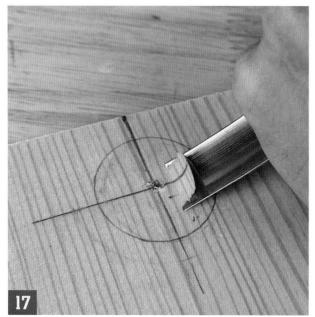

17. Using an appropriately sized and shaped carving gouge (a #6 sweep at about 15mm is ideal), make your first cut inside the circle. Do this by pushing the gouge down and toward the center hole. Make sure you are far from your boundary line at this point. Once the gouge reaches the center, try and break the chunk of wood off if it doesn't by itself.

18. Advance around the circle, making another cut toward the center hole. Continue turning your lid and making cuts toward the center, increasing the depth of cut and getting closer to your boundary lines as you go. As you work, try and get a feel for which cuts produce the cleanest surface. Pay attention to the direction your gouge is moving in relation to the wood grain. This will help you identify the most efficient and effective way of carving.

19. Complete the carving. As you continue to carve, you will get closer and closer to your boundary lines and the bottom of the hole you drilled in Step 16. When you are approaching the end, start making lighter cuts. The goal now should be to clean up any bad tearout and get the carving as circular as possible. Your final cuts should be right up against your boundary lines. Take a lot of time making sure these are as crisp as possible.

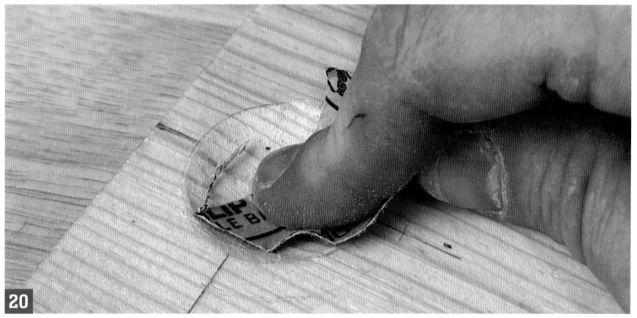

20

20. Take a small piece of sandpaper, and use your finger or thumb to sand inside the depression. Don't get carried away here, and make sure you aren't altering the circular shape of the carving. Using the lightest grit you need and continually checking your progress is a good idea.

21

21. Apply the finishing touches to the box and lid. You may need to finesse the fit of the lid a bit with a shoulder plane. I like to apply a light chamfer with a block plane to all box edges to ease things up, as well. Prepare and sand all surfaces, and apply a finish of your choice.

Miniature Dovetailed Chest

If you've been following the plans in this book so far, you may have noticed that the projects are arranged in order of difficulty, introducing new techniques and concepts along the way. This final standard box is meant to be a culmination of all you've learned so far. We're going to push your newly acquired box-making skills to the limit.

The sheer number of parts to this box may make it intimidating. There are a lot of individual components that need to be made precisely for the entire piece to come together. But don't worry! Most of the work in here you will have already encountered in previous projects, and we'll tackle things in small, easily digestible steps to stay focused. And, of course, I'll share tips I've picked up that make the process go a lot more smoothly.

The box is admittedly not entirely my own design. It's a modified version of one made by woodworker Christian Becksvoort, who himself modified it from historical Shaker designs. It's intended to be a miniaturized version of a full-size blanket chest, complete with all the traditional Shaker details—a plinth, cove molding, and of course, dovetails galore. The great thing about that is you'll pick up a lot of skills that can be used in other projects, including full-size furniture pieces. In addition to cutting dovetails, we'll go over making and installing molding, fitting a box to a plinth, making a frame and panel top, and mortising hinges. Practicing and honing these skills on a small box like this will undoubtedly help you be more prepared when you are ready to take on something bigger. I myself didn't build a full-size blanket chest until I had a few of these smaller boxes under my belt, and the experience undoubtedly helped.

This project has quite a few measurements that are critical to get everything to work right, so stick to the plans as much as possible and confirm the location of joinery, grooves, etc. before cutting anything. Also, try to resist the urge to cut costs and use cheaper hinges. They are much harder to install and very rarely deliver results worthy of fine furniture. This miniature dovetailed chest not only serves as a practice piece for enhancing precision and skill in fine joinery but also as a stylish organizer perfect for storing valuables or family heirlooms. Its thoughtful design, inspired by traditional Shaker craftsmanship, ensures it fits seamlessly into any home décor, while providing a practical storage solution.

Tools

- Combination square
- Dovetail saw
- Dividers
- Chisels, ¼"–1" (6–25mm)
- Marking gauge
- Fret or coping saw
- Mallet
- Bevel gauge
- Marking knife
- Block plane
- Jack plane
- Shoulder plane (optional)
- Router table
- Palm router
- F-clamps
- Strap clamp
- Vise
- ¼" (6mm) straight flute or spiral upcut router bit
- ⅛" (3mm) upcut spiral router bit
- Pencil
- Razor blade
- Measuring tape
- Smoothing plane
- Band saw
- Table saw
- Fine cut saw
- Drill press
- 2" (51mm)-diameter sanding drum
- ½" (13mm) cove router bit
- ¼" (6mm) drill bit
- ⅜" (10mm) brad point drill bit
- Shooting board
- Spring clamps
- Lathe
- Roughing gouge
- Spindle gouge
- Open-ended wrench
- Parting tool
- Trim router

Materials:

- White pine, ⁹⁄₁₆" (1.4cm) thick
- White pine, ½" (1.3cm) thick
- Cherry, ¼" (6.4mm) thick and 1" (2.5cm) thick
- Walnut, ¾" (1.9cm) thick and ⅜" (9.5mm) thick
- Baltic birch plywood, ¼" (6.4mm) thick
- Pair of box hinges; I use Brusso brand (product no. JB101)
- Decorative fabric, about 9" x 13" or (22.9 x 33cm)
- Spray adhesive
- Wood glue
- Blue painter's tape
- Finish, such as paste wax
- Sandpaper
- Masking tape
- Double-sided tape
- Brad nail
- Screws

Skill Building

This project will guide you through the following techniques:

- How to make a frame and panel box top/bottom

- How to plan and fit a drawer

- How to cut, fit, and troubleshoot hinge mortises

- How to create your own molding

This project utilizes dovetail joints and features a plinth and drawers. Plans can be found on pages 144–46.

Section	Material	Part	Qty.	Dimensions	Notes
CUT LIST					
Main Box	White Pine	Box sides	2	⁹⁄₁₆" x 6 ½" x 13" (1.4 x 16.5 x 33cm)	
Main Box	White Pine	Box sides	2	⁹⁄₁₆" x 7" x 9" (1.4 x 17.8 x 22.9cm)	
Main Box	Plywood	Bottom	1	¼" x 8 ⅜" x 12⅜" (6.4mm x 21.3 x 31.4cm)	
Plinth	White Pine	Plinth sides	2	⁹⁄₁₆" x 2" x 14 ⅛" (1.4 x 5.1 x 35.9cm)	
Plinth	White Pine	Plinth sides	2	⁹⁄₁₆" x 2" x 10⅛" (1.4 x 5.1 x 25.7cm)	
Drawer	White Pine	Drawer sides	2	⁹⁄₁₆" x 2⅝" x 12³⁄₁₆" (1.4 x 6.7 x 31cm)	Intentionally oversized in width
Drawer	White Pine	Drawer back	1	⁹⁄₁₆" x 2⅝" x 8" (1.4 x 6.7 x 20.3cm)	Intentionally oversized in width and length
Drawer	Cherry	Drawer front	1	1" x 2⅝" x 8" (2.5 x 6.7 x 20.3cm)	Intentionally oversized in width and length
Drawer	White Pine	Drawer stop	1	³⁄₁₆" x ½" x 3 ½" (4.8mm x 1.3 x 8.9cm)	
Drawer	Walnut	Turning blank	1	¾" x ¾" x 6" (1.9 x 1.9 x 15.2cm)	
Drawer	Plywood	Bottom	1	¼" x 7 ¼" x 11 ¹¹⁄₁₆" (6.4mm x 18.4 x 29.7cm)	
Drawer	White Pine	Frame stock	4	⅝" x 1⅛" x 13" (1.6 x 2.9 x 33cm)	Intentionally oversized in length
Top	Cherry	Panel	1	¼" x 9 ¾" x 7" (6.4mm x 24.8 x 17.8cm)	Intentionally oversized in width and length
Top	Walnut	Lid lift	1	⅜" x ⅞" x 2 ¼" (9.5mm x 2.2 x 5.7cm)	Intentionally oversized in length
Top	White Pine	Drawer support	2	½" x 1½" x 10 ⅛" (1.3 x 3.8 x 25.7cm)	Intentionally oversized in length
Misc	White Pine	Drawer support	2	½" x 1½" x 9⅛" (1.3 x 3.8 x 23.2cm)	Intentionally oversized in length
Misc	White Pine	Glue blocks	4	½" x ½" x 2 ½" (1.3 x 1.3 x 6.4cm)	
Misc	White Pine	Molding blank	1	½" x 4" x 30" (1.3 x 10.2 x 76.2cm)	
Nominal Finished Size: 9½" x 10⅛" x 14⅛" (24.1 x 25.7 x 35.9cm)					

1. Cut all the parts out according to the provided cut list. Then, gather all the materials for the main box and ensure that all stock is flat and square. Using the plans at the back of the book, mark the location of the dovetails on the tail boards. Pay special attention here. The dovetails at the front of the box are laid out differently than the back (and also have a straight instead of angled cut on one end) to accommodate the drawer.

2. Cut the dovetails as described on pages 22–26 and cover the endgrain of the tail boards with blue painter's tape. Take note that the front pin board and the rear pin board have different widths. When transferring the tails on the rear pin board, make sure to align the pin and tail boards at the bottom edge, not the top edge. When transferring the tails on the front pin board, make sure to align the bottom of the pin board with the straight cut on the tail board (i.e. the top of the drawer opening).

3. Cut the pins as described on pages 27–28. When all pins are cut, assemble and fit all four box sides. With the box assembled, turn it upside down and clamp it in a vise, if possible. Using a smoothing or jack plane, level the three sides of the box bottom. For instructions on why and how to do this, see the sidebar on page 74 in Two-Tone Sliding Lid Dovetail Box project.

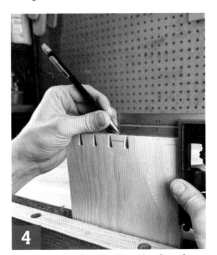

4. Using the dimensions in the plans, mark the locations for the bottom groove stops on the face of the tail boards. On the endgrain of the tail boards, mark the location of the bottom groove. You only need to do this for one of the tail boards. We'll use it to set up the router table and rout both boards.

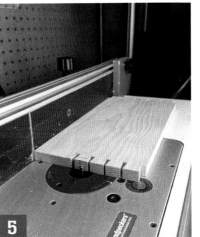

5. Chuck a ¼" (6mm) straight flute or spiral upcut bit in your router table. Using the bottom groove location you marked in the previous step, set the router fence. Place some masking tape on the fence in front of the bit. Using a combination square, mark the extremes of the router bit on the masking tape.

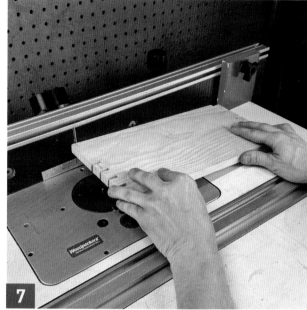

6. Take the tail board you marked in Step 4, and place the bottom edge against the router fence. Place the board so that the router bit will go past the groove stop line on your tail board just a bit. The geometry of the router bit requires this. Otherwise, the groove will not be long enough. With the board still in place, clamp a stop block to your router table fence against the opposite end of the tail board. Repeat this step for the opposite side of the router table fence using the other end of the tail board.

7. Ensure that your fence and stops are firmly locked. Raise the router bit about ⅛" (3.2mm) from the table and turn the router on. Place the right end of the tail board against the right stop, and slowly drop the board onto the spinning router bit. Slowly push the board from right to left until you reach the left stop. Turn off the router, remove the tail board, raise the bit slightly, and repeat until you are at full depth on both tail boards. *Important: Make sure you are routing with the bottom edge against the fence!*

8. Using the same fence settings, rout the bottom through grooves in only the rear pin board. (The stops will be well out of the way.) Reassemble the box, and use a marking knife to mark where the grooves in the tail boards meet the front pin board. I only mark the bottom of the groove to keep things easy to follow. Disassemble the box and transfer this mark to the endgrain on the front tail board. Clearly mark the waste side and use this to reset your router fence. Rout a groove to full depth.

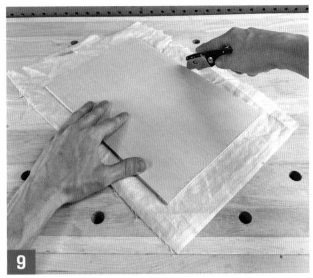

9. Spray adhesive on one side of the plywood false bottom (see cut list) and the underside of the decorative fabric. Wait about 30 seconds for the adhesive to get tacky, then press the box bottom onto the underside of the fabric. Apply firm pressure and trim the fabric to the plywood using a razor blade. For tips on lining a box bottom with fabric, see page 43 in Cherry Keepsake Box project.

10. Prepare for glue up (see page 77). Then, spread glue on the pin walls of the same side of both pin boards and attach the corresponding tail board. With the pin boards facing up on your bench, spread wood glue in the center inch (2.5cm) or so of the false bottom groove on both pinboards.

11. Slide in the false bottom. Since the bottom is plywood, we don't need to worry about undersizing it and allowing for wood movement like in earlier projects. Spread glue on the remaining exposed pin walls and attach the other tail board. Apply clamps to the tails (or cauls, if using) until the joint fully closes. Check for square by measuring corner to corner. If the distance between the corners isn't the same, skew your clamps slightly and keep checking the corner-to-corner measurement. This can take a bit of trial and error.

12. While the glue for the box is drying, gather the parts for the drawer support frame. Since this frame will be glued directly to the bottom of the box (a long-grain-to-long-grain joint), we can rely on simple butt joints to keep it together temporarily. Spread glue on the endgrain of the long frame pieces and clamp the frame together, making sure everything is aligned properly. Allow the glue to set for at least 30 minutes.

13. After the glue for both the box and the frame have set, remove all clamps and spread a bead of glue along the bottom three edges of the box bottom. Place the frame on the bottom of the box, making sure to align it flush with the end of the drawer opening. Since the frame is slightly oversized, it should overhang the other three sides just a bit. Apply clamps and allow the glue to set.

14. After about 30 minutes, remove all clamps and use a block or smoothing plane to flush up the frame overhang with the box sides. See Simple Keepsake Box with Lift Lid project (page 34) for tips on flush planing. This is also a good time to clean up all the dovetail joints on the box with a block or smoothing plane.

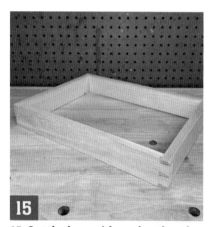

15. Set the box aside and gather the four pieces from the cut list for the plinth. Using the plans at the back of the book, mark the location for the dovetails on the tail boards. Cut the tails, transfer to the pin boards, and cut the pins. These are fairly standard dovetails, so at this point, much explanation isn't needed. At the end of the process, you should end up with a "box" that resembles the picture above.

16. Using the plans at the end of the book, mark the location of the curve cut on one of pin boards and one of the tail boards. Apply some double-sided tape to the back, and affix the pin boards together and the tail boards together, ensuring everything is aligned.

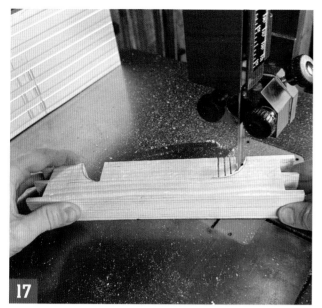

17. Head over to the band saw and cut the curves on the pin and tail boards. Make sure you stay about ⅛" (1.6mm) away from your line. Depending on the width of the blade you have in your saw, you may have to get creative at chipping away material. Don't worry too much about leaving a ragged surface if that's the case; we'll clean it up in the next step.

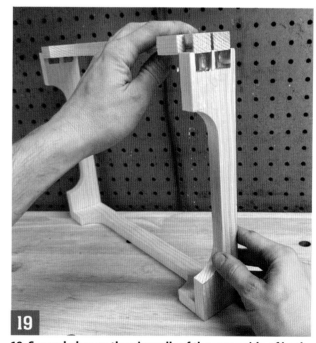

18. Chuck a 2" (51mm) diameter sanding drum that's at least 2" (5.1cm) long into the drill press and bring the table all the way up. Elevate the pin boards on a piece of ½" (1.3cm) thick scrap, and sand away material until you reach your pencil line. Take them apart and discard the double-sided tape.

19. Spread glue on the pin walls of the same side of both pin boards and attach the corresponding tail board. With the pin boards facing up on your bench, spread wood glue on the remaining exposed pin walls and attach the other tail board. Apply clamps to the tails (or cauls, if using) until the joint fully closes. Check for square by measuring corner to corner, and correct, if necessary.

Making Your Own Molding

One of the great features of this box is the cove molding that runs along the top edge of the plinth. It helps hide gaps, adds some visual appeal, and provides an additional surface to glue the box and plinth together. Its purpose is both decorative and structural. And it's something that you'll want to know how to make yourself, so you can incorporate it in future projects.

Start by gathering the molding blank from the cut list. This is the stock we'll be ripping individual

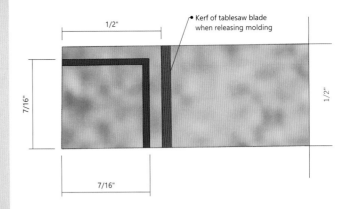

This diagram shows how to mark up the end of a board to cut molding.

Begin by making a test cut on the molding blank.

Rip the molding from the blank.

strips of molding from. In the diagram above right, the blue lines mark the extremes for where we want the cove cut to be—that is, we want to retain about 1/16" (1.6mm) of flat on the show surfaces. Make the same markings on one end of your molding stock board.

At the router table, chuck a 1/2" (13mm) cove bit, and set the fence so that is roughly centered over the bit. Raise the bit and adjust the fence until the extremes of the cove bit just touch the guidelines on the endgrain. I do this by making test cuts on the first few inches of the board, slightly adjusting after each cut until everything is just right.

Once you are satisfied with your router table settings, run the full edge of the board across the bit. Take the board to the table saw and set the fence to

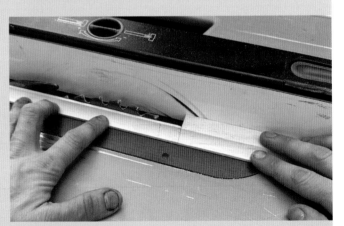

Use the first piece of molding to set the fence for subsequent cuts.

your guideline, remembering to have the molding release on the side of the blade that is not facing the fence.

Return to the router table and run the newly fresh edge of the board across the molding bit. Return to the table saw and reset the fence, using the first piece of molding you cut as a guide to get the correct width. Rip another piece of molding.

For this project, we only need two pieces of molding, but if you needed more, you would simply continue routing and ripping.

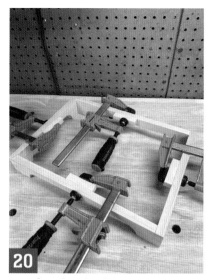

20. After the glue has set, remove all clamps and gather the glue blocks from the cut list. Spread a bead of wood glue along one face of a block, and clamp it in place on the inside wall of the plinth, roughly centered along its length (the precise location doesn't matter). Take your time and ensure that it is flush with the edge of the plinth. Repeat this for all four glue blocks.

21. After the glue has set, remove all clamps and spread a bead of glue on the top edge of all four glue blocks. Take the box and place it on top of the plinth, making sure it is properly centered. If you notice a small gap between the box and plinth, don't worry. That will be hidden by the molding. Apply clamps with light clamping pressure. Gravity will do most of the work here.

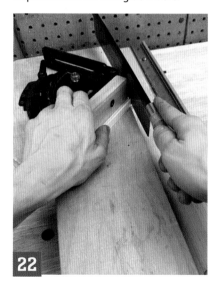

22. Gather your molding and make mitered cuts on both ends. Make sure that the miters are facing in the correct direction. When doing this, you want two pieces to be about 14½" (36.8cm) and two to be about 10½" (26.7cm) when measured from point to point.

23. Set a variable angle shooting board fence to 45 degrees. Or, if you prefer, add an auxiliary 45-degree fence to a standard shooting board. Then, trim the ends of the molding with a plane. Take one of the long pieces of molding and check the length against a long edge of the box. You want the molding to be exact in length. The inside corners of the molding should just touch the outside corner of the box. Achieve this by slowly trimming the molding at the shooting board and repeating checking the length.

24. Spread a bead of glue along the top edge of the plinth and bottom edge of the box and set the molding in place. Using various sized spring clamps, clamp the molding to the box. You may have to adjust the clamps a bit to ensure that pressure is being applied to both the plinth and the box.

25. After the glue for the first molding piece has set, trim the two shorter pieces of molding to the same size as in step 23. These are the ones applied to the short sides of the box. This time, you'll be able to rest one end of the molding against the already installed piece on the box when checking the length, so it should be much easier. When gluing and attaching these molding pieces, follow the same process as in step 24, but this time, add a bit of glue on the molding endgrain and focus clamping pressure where the molding pieces meet to ensure a gapless miter.

26. After the glue for the second and third molding pieces have set, trim the ends of the remaining long molding piece on the shooting board, keeping the piece over length. With the molding pressed firmly against the box, press one end of it against the already installed molding. You will have to bend the molding to achieve this since, it will be oversized, but it should have enough flex to do this comfortably.

27. Apply a piece of blue painter's tape to increase the molding angle. In the step photo, the angle of the molding piece needs to slightly increase. I do this by applying a piece of blue painter's tape to my shooting board fence at the end furthest from my plane (if the angle had to decrease, I would apply the tape to the end closest to my plane). With the altered fence, trim the molding piece and recheck the miter joint. Continue applying blue painter's tape, trimming, and checking until the miter is gapless. After you have set one end of the molding, repeat the process in steps 25 and 26 for the other end. Once the proper miter angle for the second end is set, trim the molding piece to size until it just fits in place. Apply a bead of glue and clamp the same as in step 24.

28. Gather the parts for the drawer. Check the width of a drawer side against the opening in the box—at this point, it should be too wide to fit in. Use a pencil to roughly mark the width of the drawer side, and trim to this width on the table saw or band saw. At this point, you still want it to fit tight, so sneak up on your cut and repeatedly check. Once you've achieved the correct width, rip all four drawer parts.

29. Check the drawer front against the opening in the box. At this point, it should be too long to fit. Slowly trim the drawer front to length using a plane and shooting board, repeatedly checking the fit until the drawer front snugly fits into the opening on the box. Trim the drawer back to match the length of the drawer front.

30. Using the plans at the back of the book, mark the location for the dovetails on the tail boards. Note that the rear tails and front tails are very different to accommodate the drawer bottom. Cut the tails, transfer to the pin boards, and cut the pins. These are fairly standard half-blind dovetails, so at this point, much explanation isn't needed. If you need a refresher on cutting half-blind dovetails, see the section on joints (page 16). At the end of the process, you should end up with a "box" that resembles the picture above.

31. Using a smoothing or jack plane, level the bottom of the drawer. Chuck a ¼" (6mm) upcut spiral bit into your router, and set the router table fence to cut the bottom groove in the appropriate location. Since the front of the drawer has a half-blind joint and the bottom will slide in from the back, you can rout through grooves on both the pin and tail boards. Rout the groove to the appropriate depth on all four pieces.

32. At the band saw (or table saw), rip the drawer back piece to final width. You ultimately want the bottom edge of the back piece to be flush with the top edge of the groove in the drawer sides. This will allow the bottom to slide in from the back. The easiest way to do this is to just set your band saw fence so that the entirety of the groove (and no more!) is removed.

33. Apply glue to the pin walls of the drawer back and front, and attach the corresponding tail boards. With these boards facing up, spread glue on the remaining pin walls and attach the other tail board. Secure with clamps until the joint closes, then check for square by measuring diagonally and adjust, if needed. Following the same procedure as in step 9, prepare a ¼" (6.4mm) Baltic birch plywood piece for the bottom. Slide it into place from the back; trim, if necessary. Once dry, remove clamps and secure the bottom with a brad nail to the drawer back's bottom edge.

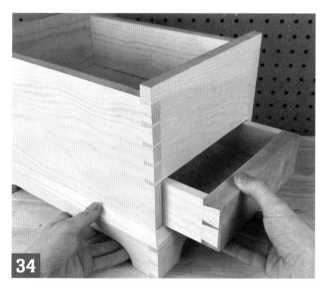

34. Try to fit the drawer into the opening on the box. At this point, you may find it is too tight. This is what we were hoping for when we sized the drawer parts. Lightly plane the drawer sides and top edge, repeatedly checking the fit to identify any sticking points. You really want to be patient here. Make very light passes with your plane and be very studious when determining which areas need to be taken down. You ultimately want the drawer to move freely in and out of the opening, but have a tight, even reveal to avoid sloppiness.

35. Glue the drawer stop. Once the drawer freely moves, and you are satisfied with the reveal around the edge of the front when closed, glue the pine drawer stop to center of the drawer back using a bit of CA glue. Reinsert the drawer in the box. If you followed the dimensions in the cut list, you should notice that the drawer front extends slightly past the edges of the box.

36. Remove the drawer and plane the drawer stop. The goal is to remove just enough material so that the drawer front is perfectly flush with the edges of the box when closed. Make only a few light plane passes, check the fit in the box, and repeat until everything is flush.

37. Mark the center of both ends of the walnut turning blank specified in the cut list, and drill a shallow hole with a ¼" (6mm) drill bit. Using the holes you just drilled, mount the blank on the lathe with a spur drive and live center, and use a roughing gouge to turn the blank to round.

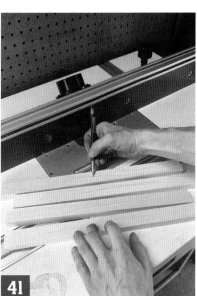

38. Following the same process in the Curly Maple Trinket Box with Ebony Pull project (page 54), use a ⅜" (1cm) open-ended wrench to establish a tenon on one end of the blank. After the tenon is set, use a spindle gouge to shape the pull to your desired profile. You can use the plans in the back of the book as a guide, or use your imagination. As long as the tenon remains the correct size you won't have problems.

39. After you've shaped the pull to your liking, sand through the grits with the lathe on. Before I switch grits, I'll turn the lathe off and sand briefly along the grain to remove any cross-grain scratches. Use the parting tool again to carefully bring the waste sections at both ends of the pull down to about ³⁄₁₆" (4.8mm).

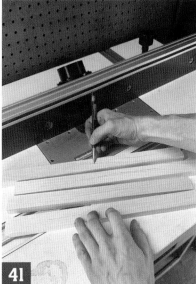

40. Use a fine cut saw or dovetail saw to cut the pull free from the blank, and clean up any unsightly nub at the top with a chisel. Mark the center of the drawer front, and using a ⅜" (10mm) brad point drill bit, drill a hole ½" (1.3cm) deep. Apply glue to the tenon of the pull, and insert it in the hole. Allow the glue to fully set before using the drawer again.

41. Gather the top frame stock pieces from the cut list, and use a pencil to mark one face on each piece. Chuck a ¼" (6mm) upcut spiral bit in your router, and use one of the frame stock pieces to set the router table fence so that the bit is roughly centered on its edge. Making sure that the face you marked is against the fence, rout one edge of all four frame pieces to final depth. Remember to make light passes and raise the bit only slightly between them.

42. Make mitered cuts on both ends of all the frame pieces. Make sure that the miters are facing in the correct direction. When doing this, you want two pieces to be about 12⅛" (30.8cm) and two to be about 9¼" (23.5cm) when measured from point to point.

43. Trim the ends of the frame pieces at a shooting board. Take one of the long pieces and check the length against a long side of the box. You want the frame piece to be just a bit shorter than the length between the two ends created by the side pieces. Make both long pieces this size. Take one of the short pieces and check is against a short side. You want this frame piece to be exactly the width of the box. Make both short pieces this size.

44. Check the dimensions needed for the panel by measuring the length of the groove in one short frame piece and one long frame piece. The long frame piece runs along the width of the panel, so make sure to make the panel about ¹⁄₁₆–⅛" (3.2–6.4mm) smaller along this dimension to allow for wood movement. Trim the panel to these dimensions.

45. Spread glue on the endgrain of both ends of the long frame pieces and in the center of the section of the panel that will sit in the grooves. Fit both long frame pieces onto the panel (attempting to keep the panel more or less centered), then fit on the short frame pieces. Wrap a strap clamp around the frame and apply enough pressure for all the miters to close up.

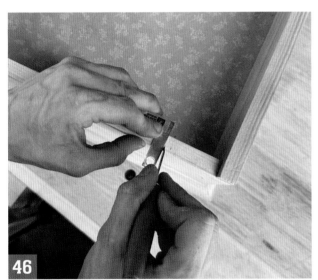 

46. Set a square on the back edge of the box, about 2" (5.1cm) from the side, and strike a line with a marking knife. Repeat on the other side. Place your marking knife in the line you made with the flat side facing the center of the box. Open a hinge, turn it upside down, and butt it up against the back of the box and your marking knife. Making sure the leaf is flat and firmly pressed against the edge of the box, score a line around it with your marking knife. Repeat on the other side.

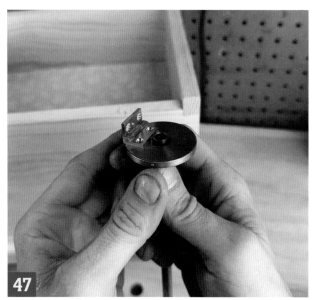

47. Set an open hinge on the fence of your marking gauge and adjust the cutter until it is just a tad beyond the thickness of the leaf. Use this setting to make a small line on the back of the box where the hinges will be located. Chuck a ⅛" (3mm) upcut spiral bit in a trim router and place it on the back edge of the box. Set the bit depth to the line you just made with the marking gauge, and rout the mortise for the hinges, making sure to stay about 1/16" (1.6mm) from your knife lines. *Note: If you find your router is tipping too much for your liking, you can always use double-sided tape to add a support block. See page 47 for an example.*

48. Finish off the walls of the mortises with a chisel. Test the fit of both hinges to make sure they fully seat. It's very easy for small pieces of waste to get in the way and mess things up really badly. You want to make sure the hinge sits just a hair below the edge. Otherwise, the lid won't close properly.

49. Set the lid on top of the box and make sure it is able to freely occupy the space between the sides. If it's too tight, lightly plane the edges of the top until it fits with a bit of play. Adjust the lid until it is flush with the front and back and centered between the sides. To make sure it is perfectly centered, slip some cardstock of the same thickness between the lid and the box on both sides until everything is snug.

50. Set the marking knife firmly against the side of one of the walls of a hinge mortise, and strike a line on the edge of the lid in the exact same location. Do the same for the other hinge mortise. Remove the lid and use a combination square to transfer the marks you just made to the underside of the lid (where the hinge mortises for the lid will be).

51. Repeat steps 46–48 to cut the mortises for the hinges. Before installing the hinges, I like to check and make sure everything will close properly by doing a "dry fit" without the screws. This helps me diagnose any issues with the mortises that could keep the lid from fully closing.

52. Use the marking knife and combination square to mark the outline of the lid lift on the underside front edge of the box lid. Make a mark ½" (1.3cm) long 4 ⅞" (12.4cm) from each edge, and then connect the marks. Adjust your trim router (still with the ⅛" (3mm) upcut spiral bit) so the bit projects ⁵⁄₁₆" (7.9mm), and rout out the mortise for the lid lift. Finish the walls with a chisel, trim the lid lift to length at the shooting board, and glue it into the mortise. After the glue has set, the lid lift will sit a bit proud of the box lid. Plane it flush using a block plane. *Note: For more detailed steps on how to mortise and install a lid lift, see pages 46–47.*

53. Drill pilot holes for the hinges, and then screw them in place on the box. Then, attach the hinges to the lid. Surface the exterior of the box and apply your finish of choice. For my box, I kept things as simple as possible and applied just a light coat of paste wax.

Catchall Tray with Marquetry

As I've stated previously, one of the great things about box-making is that once you become comfortable with a particular form or style, it can become a blank canvas for you to experiment and acquire new woodworking skills. This project is intended to provide you with an opportunity for just that.

Even though this tray is constructed with dovetail joints—a feature which alone would be enough—we'll push things further, introducing some gentle curves and soft edges to make it more inviting to hold. Getting comfortable with cutting curves and making them identical on box sides can be tricky at first, but I'll show you a simple trick that makes the process much easier.

Since this "box" doesn't have a top, it only makes sense that we try and add a bit of visual interest to the bottom. Double-bevel marquetry may seem intimidating at first, but once you practice some very basic sawing techniques, the process is surprisingly simple. We'll keep things simple and use a pattern that only requires one cut. I promise that, once you get the hang of it, you'll quickly want to move onto more intricate and challenging patterns!

Marquetry requires a few specialized tools, but luckily all of them are fairly inexpensive and easy enough to obtain from numerous online retailers. You'll need a marquetry table (or "donkey") to do all the cutting on, but I'll show you how to throw one together quickly with just a few scraps of plywood.

This versatile catchall tray not only serves as a practical storage solution but also as a beautiful display piece, perfect for showcasing your newly acquired marquetry skills. Ideal for holding keys, jewelry, or even as a decorative desk organizer, this project combines utility with artistic craftsmanship, enhancing any home décor.

Tools

- Combination square
- Dovetail saw
- Dividers
- Chisels, ¼"–1" (6–25mm)
- Marking gauge
- Fret or coping saw
- Mallet
- Bevel gauge
- Marking knife
- Block plane
- Jack plane/smoothing plane
- Router table
- F-clamps
- Deep-throat fret saw
- Pin vise
- #69 drill bits
- Marquetry donkey
- Band saw
- Router
- #2/0 jewelers saw blades (make sure to get a bunch—you'll likely break at least a few)
- ¼" (6mm) straight flute or spiral upcut router bit
- ½" (13mm) brad point drill bit
- ¼" (6mm) bearing-guided roundover router bit
- Drill press
- 1" (25mm)-diameter sanding drum
- Bench vise
- ½" (13mm) upcut spiral or straight flute cutter router bit
- Pencil
- Stylus
- Shooting board

Materials

- Koa, ⁷⁄₁₆" (2.2cm) thick
- Red oak veneer, ¹⁄₁₆" (1.6mm) thick
- Cherry veneer, ¹⁄₁₆" (1.6mm) thick
- Poplar veneer, ¹⁄₁₆" (1.6mm) thick
- Baltic birch plywood, ⅛" (3.2mm) thick
- Baltic birch plywood, ½" (1.3cm) thick
- Wood glue
- Tracing paper
- Carbon paper
- Blue painter's tape
- Finish
- Sandpaper
- Masking tape
- Double-sided tape

Skill Building

This project will guide you through the following techniques:

- Cutting and refining curves on the band saw
- Simple marquetry
- Carving edge profiles

This project utilizes dovetail joints and features simple marquetry. Plans can be found on page 147. Marquetry pattern on page 150.

Material	Part	Quantity	Dimensions	Notes
CUT LIST				
Koa	Sides	2	⁷⁄₁₆" x 2" x 10" (1.1 x 5.1 x 25.4cm)	
Koa	Sides	2	⁷⁄₁₆" x 3" x 4¼" (1.1 x 7.6 x 10.8cm)	
Red Oak	Veneer Sheet	1	¹⁄₁₆" x 4" x 9¾" (1.6mm x 10.2 x 24.8cm)	Intentionally oversized
Poplar	Veneer Sheet	1	¹⁄₁₆" x 4" x 9¾" (1.6mm x 10.2 x 24.8cm)	Intentionally oversized
Cherry	Veneer Sheet	1	¹⁄₁₆" x 4" x 9¾" (1.6mm x 10.2 x 24.8cm)	Intentionally oversized
Baltic Birch	Plywood Bottom	1	⅛" x 4" x 9¾" (3.2mm x 10.2 x 24.8cm)	Intentionally oversized
Baltic Birch	Marquetry Tabletop	1	½" x 4" x 8" (1.3 x 10.2 x 20.3cm)	
Baltic Birch	Marquetry Table Upright	1	½" x 4" x 12" (1.3 x 10.2 x 30.5cm)	
Nominal Finished Size: 3" x 4¼" x 10" (7.6 x 10.8 x 25.4cm)				

1. Cut all the parts out according to the provided cut list. Then, gather all materials and ensure that all stock is flat and square. Using the plans at the back of the book, mark the location of the dovetails on the tail boards.

2. Cut the dovetails as described on pages 22–26, and cover the endgrain of the pin boards with blue painter's tape. When transferring the tails on the front pin board, make sure to align the pin and tail boards at the bottom edge, not the top edge.

3. Cut the pins as described on pages 27–28. When all pins are cut, assemble and fit all four box sides. With the box assembled, turn it upside down and clamp it in a vise. Using a smoothing or jack plane, level the box bottom. For instructions on why and how to do this, see the sidebar on page 74.

4. Using the dimensions in the plans, mark the locations for the bottom groove stops on the face of the tail boards. On the endgrain of the tail boards, mark the location of the bottom groove. You only need to do this for one of the tail boards. We'll use it to set up the router table and rout both boards.

5. Chuck a ¼" (6mm) straight flute or spiral upcut bit in your router table. Using the bottom groove location you marked in the previous step, set the router fence. Place some masking tape on the fence in front of the bit. Using a combination square, mark the extremes of the router bit on the masking tape.

6. Take the tail board you marked in Step 5, and place the bottom edge against the router fence. Place the board so the router bit will go past the groove stop line on your tail board just a bit. The geometry of the router bit requires this. Otherwise, the groove will not be long enough. With the board still in place, clamp a stop block to your router table fence against the opposite end of the tail board. Repeat this step for the opposite side of the router table fence using the other end of the tail board.

7. Ensure that your fence and stops are firmly locked. Raise the router bit about ⅛" (3.2mm) from the table and turn the router on. Place the right end of the tail board against the right stop and slowly drop the board onto the spinning router bit. Slowly push the board from right to left until you reach the left stop. Turn off the router, remove the tail board, raise the bit slightly, and repeat until you are at full depth on both tail boards. *Important: Make sure you are routing with the bottom edge against the fence!* Using the same fence settings, rout the bottom through grooves in both pin boards. (The stops will be well out of the way.) Set the box parts aside and assemble all the materials and tools required for marquetry.

A Crash Course in Double-Bevel Marquetry

Since this book is primarily focused on box-making, there simply isn't enough time for me to go through the ins and outs of marquetry. The art of marquetry is a very complex subject, and the finer points can take quite a bit of time to acquire and hone. That being said, a simple one-piece pattern, such as the one for this project, can be done fairly easily with a bit of preparation and knowledge.

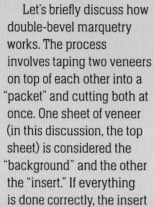

Let's briefly discuss how double-bevel marquetry works. The process involves taping two veneers on top of each other into a "packet" and cutting both at once. One sheet of veneer (in this discussion, the top sheet) is considered the "background" and the other the "insert." If everything is done correctly, the insert veneer piece should fit perfectly into the void left in the background sheet. If you simply taped your veneers together and cut them with your fret saw on a flat table, your insert veneer would be smaller than the void left in the background veneer. The reason for this is that, as you cut with the saw, material is lost to sawdust. The gap around the insert veneer and the background veneer in the image to the left is exactly equal to the width of the saw cut.

If we angle the cutting table while still ensuring that we saw straight up and down, however, things change. This creates a "bevel" on the edges of the insert piece and the void in the background piece—hence double bevel—that allows the insert piece to be fit into the background veneer from behind like a cork.

Getting this all to work properly is all about setting the cutting angle properly. The optimal cutting angle is entirely a function of the kerf of the saw blade and the thickness of the veneer you are using. This is typically found through trial and error, but if you are using ¹⁄₁₆" (1.6mm)-thick veneers and #2/0 fret saw blades, 8 degrees works well. Simply clamp your cutting table in a bench vise and tilt it 8 degrees. I find a digital angle gauge works best. Adjust the table height so that it is in line with your shoulders when you sit.

I like to set my table so that it is angled with the lower part on the left. This is a personal choice, but

Setting the table angle using a digital angle gauge.

Building a Marquetry Donkey

Marquetry requires a number of specialized tools that you likely don't have sitting around the shop. You'll need a decent deep-throat fret saw to do the pattern in this project. The saw you use to remove waste when cutting dovetails just won't suffice. You'll also need the appropriate blades and drill bits—2/0 and #69, respectively—which are much finer than those used in other woodworking tasks. You can purchase all of these (along with a pin vise to hold those tiny drill bits) easily online, but you're probably going to have to make your own marquetry table.

There are plenty of designs for a wide variety of marquetry tables online, and if you want to get really fancy, you absolutely can. But anything more than a couple of scraps of plywood is totally unnecessary for this project, so let's just stick with that.

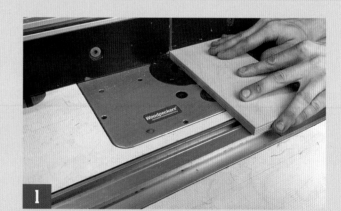

1. Gather the pieces of ½" (1.3cm) thick Baltic birch plywood specified in the cut list. At the router table, chuck a ½" (13mm) upcut spiral or straight flute cutter and set the fence about 2" (5.1cm) from the bit (you don't have to worry about being exact here). Rout a dado about ⅛" (3.2mm) deep across the short length of the shorter piece of plywood.

Double-Bevel Geometry

Void left in background veneer

Material lost from sawing, i.e. the kerf of the saw blade

Insert veneer piece

Note how the width of the insert veneer piece (at the top) is the same as the void left in the background veneer. This is due to the angle of the saw cut, which allows the insert veneer piece to be inserted from behind and eliminate any gaps from the saw kerf.

know that it affects the direction in which you will make your cuts. A table tilted to the left requires you to cut in a clockwise direction to ensure the bevel is angled in the correct direction on both your insert and background veneers.

With the tools assembled, table built, and angle set, it's time to get cutting! The great thing about double-bevel marquetry is that there are only two things you really need to remember when sawing. The first is to make sure you are sawing straight up and down, perpendicular to the ground and not your table! If you deviate from cutting straight up and down, you are altering the bevel angle on your veneers. This could result in either an insert piece that is too tight to fit in the background veneer, or one that fits with a lot of unsightly gaps.

The second is that as you are sawing, it is imperative that you keep the teeth pointed straight forward at all

times. As you saw around complex patterns, beginners have a tendency to want to move the saw blade to follow a line—do not do this! Instead, think of your saw as a stationary tool moving up and down with your dominant hand. Your non-dominant hand "feeds" the packet of veneers into the saw blade, moving it in whichever necessary direction to follow the pattern lines.

As long as you follow those basic sawing tips, you'll find it's pretty easy to get the hang of things. I strongly recommend you read through the marquetry steps in this project and practice on some scrap first. This will give you time to get the feel for proper sawing and adjusting the table angle if things are a bit off. I like to start by cutting a few practice circles in the same veneer I'll be using for my project. If my pieces are too tight, I'll decrease my cutting angle. If they are loose, I'll increase it.

An example of insert pieces that are too tight and too loose.

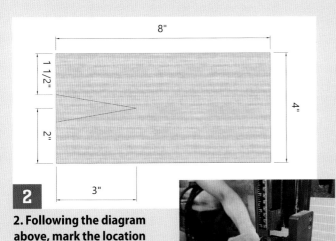

2. Following the diagram above, mark the location for the marquetry table's "bird's mouth" with a pencil. Remove it at the band saw.

3. Clamp the longer piece of plywood upright in a bench vise, and affix the shorter piece on top at the dado you cut in step one. Drill and countersink holes on the top about 1" (2.5cm) in from each edge, making sure they pass through the center of the dado and into the upright piece. Drive screws in to permanently affix the table, and you're done!

8. Copy the marquetry pattern at the end of the book onto a piece of tracing paper. Position the pattern roughly in the center of the red oak veneer sheet and tape it in place. Slip a sheet of carbon paper between the tracing paper and veneer, and use a pencil or stylus to transfer the pattern onto the veneer.

9. Turn over the red oak veneer, and secure the cherry veneer sheet to it using masking tape. Make sure the veneer sheets are tightly taped together. If they shift at all during sawing, you'll end up with unsightly gaps.

10. Using a #69 drill bit in a pin vise, drill a hole through both veneers from the top. Pay special attention to where the hole is drilled here. It is on the inside of the pattern line (i.e. the section that will be cut out) and in the middle of a slight curve. Hold your pin vise so that the drill bit is entering at an angle even steeper than your table angle (i.e. tilt the top of the pin vise to the right). This will help make sure the hole enters the cherry veneer in a section that will not be used.

Threading a Fret Saw

Hold your fret saw upside down and clamp a #2/0 blade in the side with the handle. Make sure the teeth of the blade are pointed up and toward the handle. I find it helps to rest the far end of the saw frame against the edge of the marquetry table, and the handle against my sternum.

Thread the saw blade through the hole you made in the veneers, making sure the teeth are pointing in the direction of the cut. Hold the veneer packet in your non-dominant hand and rest the frame of the fret saw on the edge of your marquetry table. Apply pressure to the handle of the fret saw with your sternum to apply tension to the fret saw frame, and with your dominant hand, secure the fret saw blade to the saw.

With the saw still between your sternum and the table, keep your non-dominant hand holding the veneer packet, and move your dominant hand to the saw handle. Carefully turn over the packet and place it on the table with the pattern facing up.

First, hold the fret saw upside down and clamp in the new blade.

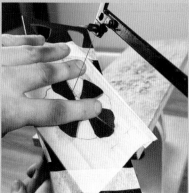

Next, thread the blade through the veneer packet (top) and flip it over onto the marquetry table (bottom).

11. Thread a #2/0 fret saw blade through the hole in the veneer packet from the back, making sure the teeth are pointing to the top of the pattern. Then, secure the blade to the saw frame. Carefully place the veneer packet with the saw threaded through flat on your cutting table with the pattern facing up.

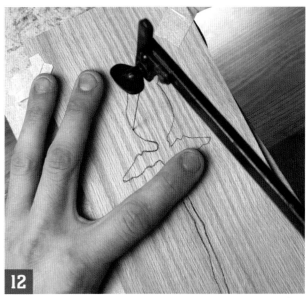

12. Before you begin sawing, take note of the location of the saw blade inside the hole. You want to make sure that the blade is all the way to the left in the hole. That way, any remnant of the hole will remain in the section you cut out. Begin sawing, remembering to keep your blade perpendicular to the floor with teeth pointing forward at all times. *Note: Remember to saw around your pattern clockwise, not counterclockwise.*

13. Continue sawing, making sure to rotate the packet of veneers as you cut and not the saw. Provide firm support with the forefinger and middle finger of your non-dominant hand as you continue cutting. As you saw, don't worry too much about staying exactly on your line. If your cut deviates, resist the urge to immediately correct it back to your line. Instead, try to incorporate the deviation into the design, and maintain fair and consistent curves in your cut.

TIP: If you find the sections that you already cut are moving around too much for your comfort, you can always unthread your saw, apply some masking tape over the already cut section, and then rethread your saw. This will help keep things more together as you continue through cutting the pattern.

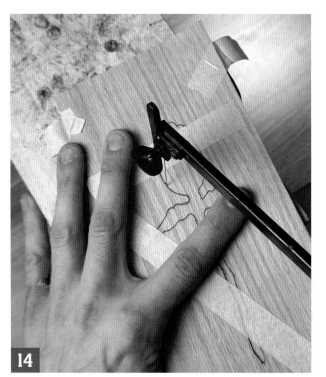 

14. As you approach the end of the cut, try to ensure that your saw will connect with the hole you drilled again on the left side, exactly where you started the cut. This part is critical. If the kerfs from the start of your cut and the end of your cut don't line up, things will look a bit off.

15. Carefully remove the pieces of red oak and cherry veneer you just cut from the veneer packet, and remove all tape. Test the fit by inserting the cherry veneer piece you just cut out into the red oak veneer from behind. Remember, if the piece is too loose, your angle wasn't steep enough. If it is too tight, your angle was too steep. Spread a thin bead of glue around the edge and permanently press it into the red oak veneer from behind.

16. Spread an ample amount of wood glue on both sides of the ⅛" (3.2mm) piece of plywood specified in the cut list. Press the veneer pattern firmly on one side and a piece of poplar veneer on the other side. Use your fingers to align both veneer sheets to one corner of the plywood packet and stretch blue painter's tape over the edges. This will help prevent things from shifting when clamped.

17. Line two scrap pieces of plywood or MDF with blue painter's tape and sandwich the veneer packet between them. Clamp the sandwich together and let the glue set for at least 30 minutes. After the glue has fully dried, remove the veneer packet from the clamps and pull off all that blue painter's tape you've used up to this point. Joint one edge of the packet on a shooting board, and then use this as a reference edge at the table saw (or stay at the shooting board) to trim the bottom to the dimensions listed in the plans.

18. Using the plans at the back of the book, mark the location of the curve cut and finger hole on one of the pin boards. Apply some double-sided tape to the back and affix the pin boards together, ensuring everything is aligned.

19. With the pin boards together, drill the finger hole using a ½" (13mm) brad point drill bit at the drill press. Then, head over to the band saw and cut the curve, making sure you stay about ¹⁄₁₆" (1.6mm) away from your line. Depending on the width of the blade you have in your saw, you may have to get creative at chipping away material. Don't worry too much about leaving a ragged surface if that's the case. We'll clean it up in the next step.

20. Back at the drill press, chuck a 1" (25mm)-diameter sanding drum that's at least 2" (5.1cm) long, and bring the table all the way up. Elevate the pin boards on a piece of ½" (1.3cm) thick scrap and sand away material until you reach your pencil line. Since all drilling, cutting, and sanding was done on both pinboards at the same time, they'll be perfectly identical. Take them apart and discard the double-sided tape.

21. At the router table, chuck a ¼" (6mm) bearing-guided roundover bit. Raise it slightly above the table and rout the top edge of one of your pin boards. Keep raising the bit very slightly and doing cuts until you reach the profile you like. It doesn't take much. Once you are satisfied, rout the top edge of both pin boards on the inside and outside, the top edge of both tail boards on the inside and out, and the edges of the finger holes on the inside and out.

22. You may find the router left a less-than-perfect surface, so use some sandpaper to cleanup your roundovers, if necessary. After preparing for glue up (see page 77 for more on this), spread glue on the pin walls of the same side of both pin boards, and attach the corresponding tail board. With the pin boards facing up on your bench, spread wood glue in the center inch or so (2.5cm) of the bottom groove in both pin boards.

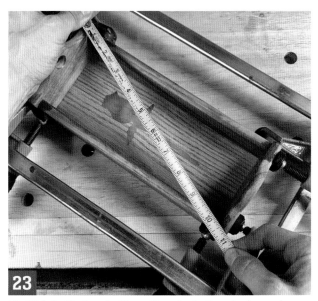

23. Slide in the box bottom. Since the bottom is plywood, we don't need to worry about undersizing it and allowing for wood movement like in earlier projects. Spread glue on the remaining exposed pin walls and attach the other tail board. Apply clamps to the tails (or cauls, if using them) until the joint fully closes. Check for square by measuring corner to corner. If the distance between the corners isn't the same, skew your clamps slightly and keep checking the corner-to-corner measurement.

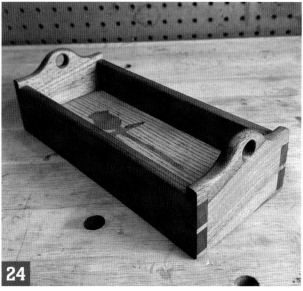

24. After the glue has finished drying, apply all finishing touches to clean up the joints and surfaces. See page 16 for how to clean up dovetails. I like to apply a light chamfer with a block plane to the bottom edges of the tray to ease things up as well. Prepare and sand all surfaces, and apply the finish of your choice.

Asymmetrical Band Saw Box

Band saw boxes are a great way to let your creativity fly. Unlike the previous projects in this book, there are much fewer rules and dimensions to follow here. All you have to do is make a few carefully sequenced cuts on the band saw, glue things up, and then you're off—the rest is up to you!

There are any number of ways to decorate your band saw box, but in this project, I'll show off some simple techniques to add texture and visual interest. But you really shouldn't be afraid to experiment here. Use it as a springboard to try something new or incorporate another of your artistic talents.

The good news is the cost of entry here is very low. All you need is a single block of wood that you likely already have sitting in the corner of your shop. Even better, this project can be started and completed in an afternoon, so you don't need to worry about blocking off a lot of time.

Band saw boxes can take many forms, so if you like this project, you should do some further research on the subject. There are some really wild designs out there that may pique your interest!

This specific band saw box, with its fluid form and textured surface, offers a stylish yet functional piece perfect for storing small personal items or serving as a unique home décor accent. Its streamlined design and the tactile appeal make it an excellent starting point for exploring more intricate and personalized box projects.

This box has no joinery, as it's all cut from a single piece of wood on the band saw. For added interest, paint it and carve in texture. Plans on page 148.

Tools
- Band saw
- Clamps
- Block plane
- Combination square
- Bevel gauge
- Pencil
- ½" (13mm) 3 TPI blade
- Rasps (optional)
- Spokeshave (optional)
- #5 sweep gouge (optional)

Materials
- Blank of poplar, 2½" x 4¼" x 7½" (6.4 x 10.8 x 19.1cm)
- Wood glue
- Finish
- Sandpaper
- Metallic paint (optional)

Skill Building

This project will
guide you through the
following techniques:

- Making boxes
  without joinery

- Adding texture
  to boxes

1. Prepare a block of wood to the listed dimensions.
Using a combination square and a bevel gauge, mark the cut lines for the top, bottom, and sides following the diagram in the plans. It's also helpful at this stage to clearly mark which pieces are the top, bottom, and sides. That will help you keep everything in order.

2. Set the fence on your band saw to the lines you marked for the top and bottom. Using an appropriate blade (I prefer a ½" (13mm) 3 TPI blade), resaw the box top and bottom off the wood blank and set aside.

3. Take the remaining portion of the wood blank, and mark the corners following the photo above. This will form the sides of the box. This will help you line up the correct parts during glue up and remove a lot of frustrating guesswork.

4. Angle your band saw table to about 7 degrees. This step is optional, but I like to do it because it causes the inner walls of the box to slope inward. With the table angled, set the fence on your band saw to meet the cut lines for the sides you drew in Step 1.

5. Carefully saw off one box side, rotate the blank, and saw off the opposing side. Set the sides aside. Rotate the remaining blank 90 degrees and set it against the fence. Make a crosscut, rotate the blank, and make a crosscut from the opposite side. At the end of this step, you should have four box sides and a much smaller remaining blank.

6. Spread glue on the ends of the short box sides and line them up with the long box sides using the marks you made in Step 3. Carefully clamp the sides together, using your fingers to feel for any mismatches at the joints. Allow the glue to set for about 30 minutes.

7. Resaw about ¼" (6.4mm) from the top (the wider part) of the remaining blank. This piece will be used to form an inset for the box top. Take the inset and check to see if it freely fits inside the box. You want only a bit of play here. If the inset is too tight, plane the ends or sides appropriately to fit.

9. Spread wood glue on the inset and press it onto the underside of the box top. Take time to line up the inset with the pencil lines you drew in the previous step. Apply clamps and allow the glue to set. While the glue for the top is drying, you can glue on the bottom. Spread a bead of wood glue along the bottom edge of the box (this will be the thicker edge if you angled your table in Step 4) and clamp the bottom on. Allow the glue to set.

8. After the glue for the sides has set, remove the clamps. Place the box upside down on the underside of the lid piece you cut in Step 2. Use a pencil to trace the inside perimeter of the box edge onto the lid.

10. Remove the clamps from the top and bottom. Using a combination square, mark a 1" (2.5cm) border around the entirety of the box top. This line serves as a reference for where the inner wall of the box is. Draw the shape of your box's outer walls between this line and the outer edge of the box top. You can get really creative here, but if you do a lot of tight curves, you might have to use a narrower band saw blade.

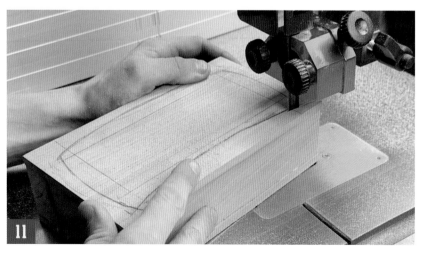

11. Use double-sided tape to affix the lid onto the box. At the band saw, carefully cut to your outer box walls. You can also choose to angle the band saw table at this point if you want the outer box walls to be angled. Just make sure you pay attention to the direction of the angle relative to your box as you cut. At the end of this step, you'll end up with a (albeit rough) finished box! How you choose to finish things from here is entirely up to you.

Finishing a Band Saw Box

One of the best things about band saw boxes is that once the general form of the box is together, the fun can really start. There are so many ways to decorate band saw boxes that I won't bother trying to list everything. Instead, I'll show you some of my personal favorites.

Creating rough sides by kissing the box against a band saw blade.

I really like the rough surface that a band saw leaves—the texture can be very pleasing. Sometimes instead of sanding the outside of my box, I use the outer edge of a running band saw blade to "kiss" it. This causes a series of vertical saw grooves to be left on the surface. I'll then apply some paint and sand it back so that it only remains in the deeper saw grooves.

If you instead choose to smooth the sides like I did for this box, it's helpful to have a lot of different finishing tools at your disposal. To handle the large sweeping

Using a block plane to refine an outside curve.

outside curve of the back of the box, I used a block plane. The short sole allows it to target high spots and leave you with a nicely faired curve.

The inside curve of the front of the box was a bit more challenging. For these situations, a woodworker's rasp (not a file!) can quickly remove the band saw marks. You can then further refine the surface with a curved bottom spokeshave to get everything nice and smooth.

To add a little texture to the top of my box, I carved small divots using a #5 sweep gouge. There are really no rules here. I just scooped out material until I liked the finished look. Since I used a metallic paint for the outside of my box, light reflects off the carving and really catches the eye.

I also never leave out the inside of a band saw box! On this one, some gold metallic paint provides a little surprise when the box is opened. If I were feeling a bit more adventurous, I could have carved the interior walls before glueing them up in Step 6 and made things really interesting.

Using a rasp to refine the box surface.

Using a spokeshave to refine the box surface.

Carving texture on the lid of the box.

Painting the inside of the box.

Padauk and Curly Maple Turned Ring Box

So far, most of the boxes we've covered in this book follow the same general form—four sides joined together with a top and a bottom. But if you have a lathe and a few accessories, it's fairly easy to branch out and explore new shapes.

In this project, I'll go over how to make a very simple turned ring box. As I've said before, I'm no master turner myself, so I tried to keep things easy here. You'll want to be familiar with general turning techniques before trying to tackle this box—namely how to turn a simple spindle. Practicing first with a few pen or pencil kits is a great way to get yourself comfortable with the lathe work involved here. But this certainly is not an advanced turning project by any means. Instead of hollowing out the inside of the box with turning chisels, we'll take the easy route and use some Forstner bits to do the heavy lifting.

As with most of the boxes in this book, you should feel free to experiment and deviate from the provided plans. As long as you stick to the critical dimensions (the hollows in the top and bottom and the bottom lip), feel free to change up the shape of the box and the pull. I didn't even know what mine was going to look like until I was finished. Regarding material, I used padauk, but I sized the box so that you can easily source any number of species of turning stock from the many online and brick-and-mortar hardwood dealers.

This turned ring box, elegant in its simplicity, offers a stylish and secure place for storing rings or small jewelry. Perfect for beginners wanting to explore turning, this project emphasizes practical skills in shaping and hollowing with easy-to-follow steps. The warm tones of the padauk wood enhance the aesthetic appeal, making it a delightful addition to any dresser or nightstand.

This box features two stunning woods, padauk and curly maple. Experiment with different wood types for varied looks. There is no joinery, as it's turned on the lathe. Plans on page 149.

Tools
- Four-jaw scroll chuck for lathe
- Drill chuck for lathe
- 1¾" (44mm) Forstner bit and 1⅝" (41mm) Forstner bit
- Lathe and turning chisels (roughing gouge, parting tool, spindle gouge, skew chisel)
- Chisels
- ¼" (6mm) drill bit
- Ruler
- Pencil
- ¼" (6mm) open-ended wrench
- Fine cut saw or dovetail saw
- Dividers
- Scissors

Materials
- Padauk turning blank, 2" (5.1cm) square
- Curly maple turning blank, ¾" (1.9cm) square
- Wood glue
- Cork liner
- Copper metallic paint
- Finish
- Sandpaper

CUT LIST			
Material	**Part**	**Quantity**	**Dimensions**
Padauk	Turning Blank	1	2" x 2" x 5½" (5.1 x 5.1 x 14cm)
Curly Maple	Turning Blank	1	¾" x ¾" x 6" (1.9 x 1.9 x 15.2cm)
Nominal Finished Size: 1 ¾" x 5" (4.5 x 12.7cm)			

1. Mark the center of both ends of the padauk turning blank specified in the cut list. Then, drill a shallow hole with a ¼" (6mm) drill bit. Using the holes you just drilled, mount the blank on the lathe with a spur drive and live center (i.e. "turning between centers").

2. With the lathe spinning at its highest speed, use a roughing gouge to turn the blank to round and about 1⅞" (4.8cm) in diameter. I like to repeatedly check to see if my blank is round by gently resting my gouge on top of the spinning blank. If it's a bumpy ride, then it isn't round yet.

3. With the lathe off, use a ruler to mark the critical locations on the blank with a pencil. Reference the marking guide in the plans. After you've made the initial markings, turn the lathe on at low speed and press your pencil against the blank where the markings are to have them transferred around the entire blank.

4. Use a parting tool to define the location of the tenons on both ends of the blank. You don't need to turn the tenons down to a specific diameter. Just make sure they are about ¼" (6.4mm) smaller than the rest of the blank, so the chuck has a nice surface to rest against.

5. After the tenons are defined, remove the blank and spur drive. Mount a four-jaw scroll chuck on the lathe. Press fit the blank between the open chuck and the live center, and then tighten the chuck. At this point, it's perfectly fine and even preferable to keep the live center engaged, so leave it in place for now.

6. Using the parting tool, turn down the middle section of the blank by about ¹⁄₁₆" (1.6mm). This is where the top and bottom of the box will be separated. Make sure not to remove too much material here or your box top won't fit well! With the left side of the parting tool resting against the edge of the left side of the blank, remove material until the two sections of the blank come apart. Do this part carefully, making sure your non-dominant hand is providing support for the right side of the blank when it releases.

7. With the top and the bottom of the box separated, we can now do the critical work of hollowing the box and fitting the lid. With the top of the box still mounted in the scroll chuck, mount a drill chuck and a 1¾" (44mm) Forstner bit in the lathe's tailstock. Turn the lathe on and slowly advance the Forstner bit until it has drilled a hole ½" (1.3cm) deep. This can be very slow going, so stay patient and try not to overwork the bit.

8. Remove the box top from the chuck and mount the box bottom. Using a 1⅝" (41mm) Forstner bit in the drill chuck, turn the lathe on and slowly advance the bit until it has drilled a hole ¾" (1.9cm) deep. With the lathe off, try to fit the box lid on the box bottom. Chances are, at this point, things won't fit. Use the parting tool to very carefully turn down the lip on the box bottom until the lid just slips over it.

9. With the box together and mounted between your scroll chuck and live center, use the parting tool to define the ends of the box. Turn these sections down so that only about ¼" (6.4mm) of material remains. These are the sections you will ultimately cut to release the box from the blank. After the ends are defined, use the roughing gouge to true up the box, making sure where the top and bottom meet is clean.

Troubleshooting

If you messed up and made the lip on the bottom of the box too small, don't panic! Your lid might not fit as tight as you'd like, but it will still be a perfectly fine box. To proceed and finish the box safely, though, you'll want to take an extra step.

What makes this box fairly easy to execute well is that you are able to turn the profile of the lid and the bottom at the same time. This is because, as you'll see in later steps, the lid is fit over the lip of the bottom, and then the box is turned. This is a fantastic method to ensure a pleasing profile, but it requires the lid to have a tight fit, otherwise, that thing will just spin like wild on the lathe.

If your lid just doesn't have a fit tight enough, all you have to do is build it up a bit. Wrapping a bit of sandpaper around it before affixing the lid may work, or if that is too thick, try a paper towel. Basically, use anything you can to build up that lip so that the lid sits on tightly. Then, you won't have any issues finishing off the box despite your mistake.

10. Use your roughing gouge, spindle gouge, skew chisel—whatever you are comfortable with—to shape the outside profile of your box. Feel free to get creative here, just remember that the right side is the top of your box and the left is the bottom!

11. Using the parting tool, turn down the top end of the box until it releases from the live center. Make sure to provide support with your non-dominant hand to make sure the box lid doesn't go flying off the lathe when things release!

12. Remove the live center from the lathe's tailstock and replace it with a drill chuck and ¼" (6mm) drill bit. Drill a hole ³⁄₁₆" (4.8mm) deep. This is the mortise to accept the tenon for the lid's pull. Reinstall the live center and engage it in the hole you just drilled. Using a skew chisel (or preferred tool), do the final shaping of the box top.

13. With the lathe on, sand through the grits until you have fully surfaced the exterior of the box. Remove the lid and sand the interior of the box and lip as well. Don't worry too much about the bottom of the box. That part gets covered with cork so nobody is going to see it.

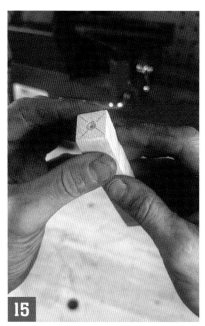

14. With only the bottom of the box mounted, engage the live center. It will go inside the box and seat in the tip of the Forstner bit hole from step 8. Using the parting tool, turn down the bottom end of the box until it releases from the live center. Provide support with your non-dominant hand to make sure the box bottom doesn't go flying off the lathe when things release. Clean up any unsightly nub that may remain on the bottom of the box with a chisel and sandpaper.

15. Mark the center of both ends of the curly maple turning blank specified in the cut list, and drill a shallow hole with the ¼" (6mm) drill bit. Using the holes you just drilled, mount the blank on the lathe with a spur drive and live center.

16. Use the roughing gouge to turn the blank to round. After the blank is round, use the parting tool to define the location of the pull's tenon. The tenon will ultimately be ¼" (6.4mm) in diameter, so try to bring the tenon down to about ⁵⁄₁₆" (7.9mm) at this stage.

17. After you have your tenon well established and oversized, gather a ¼" (6mm) open-ended wrench. With the wrench pressed against the tenon on the backside, use the parting tool carefully with one hand to reduce the size of the tenon until the open end of the wrench just fits over it.

18. Use the spindle gouge to shape the pull to your desired profile. You can use the plans in the back of the book as a guide, or use your imagination. As long as the tenon remains the correct size, you won't have problems later.

19. After you've shaped the pull to your liking, sand through the grits with the lathe on. Before I switch grits, I'll turn the lathe off and sand briefly along the grain to remove any cross-grain scratches. Use the parting tool again to carefully bring the waste sections at both ends of the pull down to about ³⁄₁₆" (4.8mm).

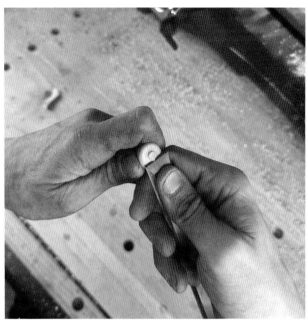

20. Use a fine cut saw or dovetail saw to cut the pull free from the blank. On the bottom of the pull, you don't need to worry about any clean up since it's just a tenon, but at the top, you'll be left with an unsightly nub. There are a lot of complicated ways of removing this, but I find just chipping it away with a chisel and cleaning things up with sandpaper to be wholly sufficient. Apply a dab of glue inside the ¼" (6.4mm) hole in the box top and press the tenon of the pull through. Wait about 30 minutes for the glue to dry.

21. To liven up the interior of the box, I like to paint the inside with some copper metallic paint. On a wood like padauk with it's striking color, a few coats may be necessary. To provide a bit of padding, I like to line the inside bottom of the box with cork. Open a set of dividers to ¹³⁄₁₆" (2.1cm) and use them to scribe a circle in some cork liner. Usually, I can get away with cutting the cork out like this, but you may need to use some scissors to finish cutting out the cork circle. After its out, a dab of wood glue will keep it affixed to the bottom of the interior of the box. Apply a finish of your choice.

Beyond the Basics

This book provides a comprehensive introduction to fine woodworking through box-making projects, equipping you with a variety of techniques in joinery, construction, and decoration. As you've progressed, these skills should now feel more accessible, and while we've covered a broad range of topics, there's still plenty to explore. Fortunately, you're well-prepared to apply these techniques to further projects, requiring only minor modifications to adapt what you've already learned.

Splines are a great place to add strength and flair. These thin, crisscrossed splines by Owen Churchill resemble stitching.

Splines

Enhance miter joints with splines to convert weak connections into strong, decorative elements, using contrasting woods and unique patterns for both durability and visual appeal. Pictured here are veneer splines in a miter joint.

Dovetails

While the projects in this book focused on evenly spaced dovetails, there's no rule saying one can't vary the spacing based on your preference and desired aesthetic.

You can take your dovetails to another level by inlaying complementary woods along the edges. These inlaid dovetails were created by Amanda Fritts.

Angled Walls

With a little bit of practice, you can cut the angled sides on a table saw and refine your angles using the mitered shooting board detailed on page 15.

Decorative Elements

Think of marquetry like painting with wood. Beginners can start with simple patterns and advance to complex images using layered veneers.

Carving designs into your boxes is a great way to add your own unique touch. Examples of masterful carving by Shea Alexander.

You're not beholden to just natural wood colors for veneers, either. Experiment with dyes and stains to capture the aesthetic you desire.

Beyond Boxes

The fundamentals taught in this book can easily transfer to making larger items, such as furniture and cabinetry. This wall cabinet I made for my wife's seed collection, while fairly complex looking, can be viewed as simply a large box divided into smaller spaces and outfitted with drawers.

You can make divided boxes by applying similar techniques as the ones taught in this book. You could easily replicate this box by following the steps to add a liner in the Bubinga Gift Box with Framed Lid project (page 48), and making a tray following the same steps in the Catchall Tray with Marquetry project (page 102). Boxes with dividers are a great entry point into cabinetry or making drawers.

This shaker blanket chest employs all the techniques we covered in this book, particularly those taught in the Miniature Dovetailed Chest project (page 82).

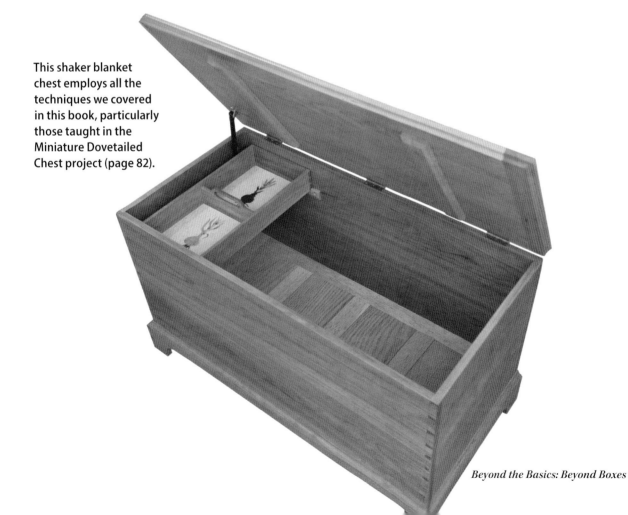

Project Plans
Standard Shooting Board

Project on page 14.

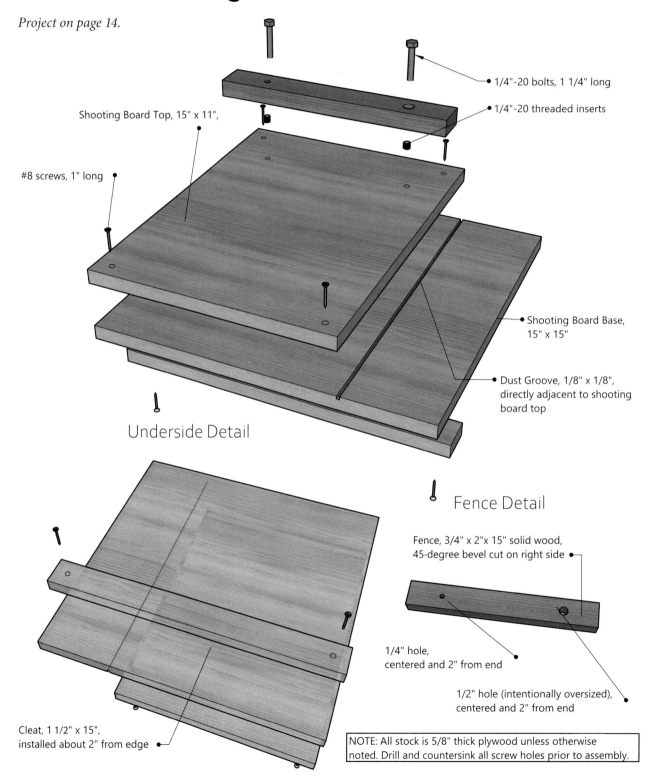

1/4"-20 bolts, 1 1/4" long

1/4"-20 threaded inserts

Shooting Board Top, 15" x 11",

#8 screws, 1" long

Shooting Board Base, 15" x 15"

Dust Groove, 1/8" x 1/8", directly adjacent to shooting board top

Underside Detail

Fence Detail

Fence, 3/4" x 2" x 15" solid wood, 45-degree bevel cut on right side

1/4" hole, centered and 2" from end

1/2" hole (intentionally oversized), centered and 2" from end

Cleat, 1 1/2" x 15", installed about 2" from edge

NOTE: All stock is 5/8" thick plywood unless otherwise noted. Drill and countersink all screw holes prior to assembly.

Mitered Shooting Board

Project on page 15.

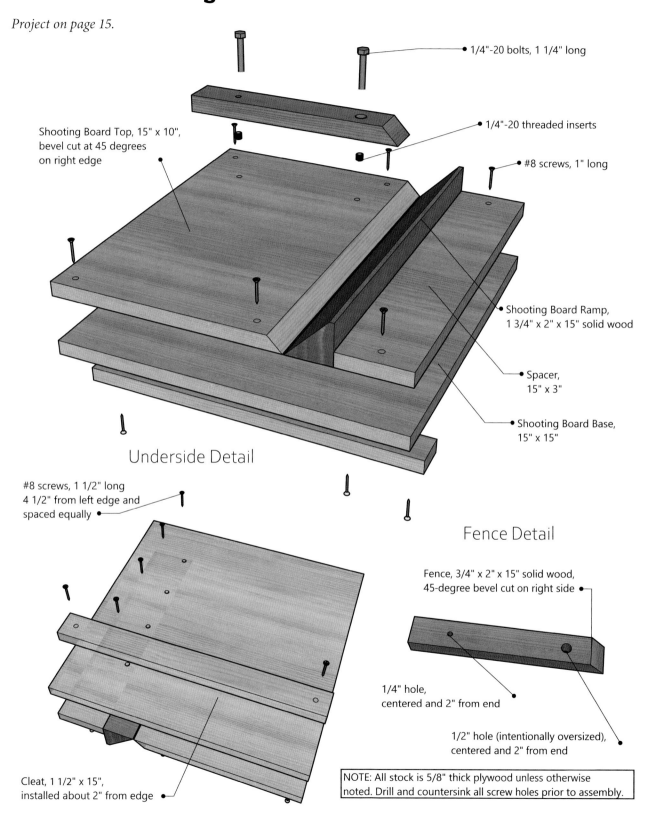

1/4"-20 bolts, 1 1/4" long

1/4"-20 threaded inserts

Shooting Board Top, 15" x 10", bevel cut at 45 degrees on right edge

#8 screws, 1" long

Shooting Board Ramp, 1 3/4" x 2" x 15" solid wood

Spacer, 15" x 3"

Shooting Board Base, 15" x 15"

Underside Detail

#8 screws, 1 1/2" long 4 1/2" from left edge and spaced equally

Fence Detail

Fence, 3/4" x 2" x 15" solid wood, 45-degree bevel cut on right side

1/4" hole, centered and 2" from end

1/2" hole (intentionally oversized), centered and 2" from end

Cleat, 1 1/2" x 15", installed about 2" from edge

NOTE: All stock is 5/8" thick plywood unless otherwise noted. Drill and countersink all screw holes prior to assembly.

Simple Pine Keepsake Box with Lift Lid

Project on page 34.

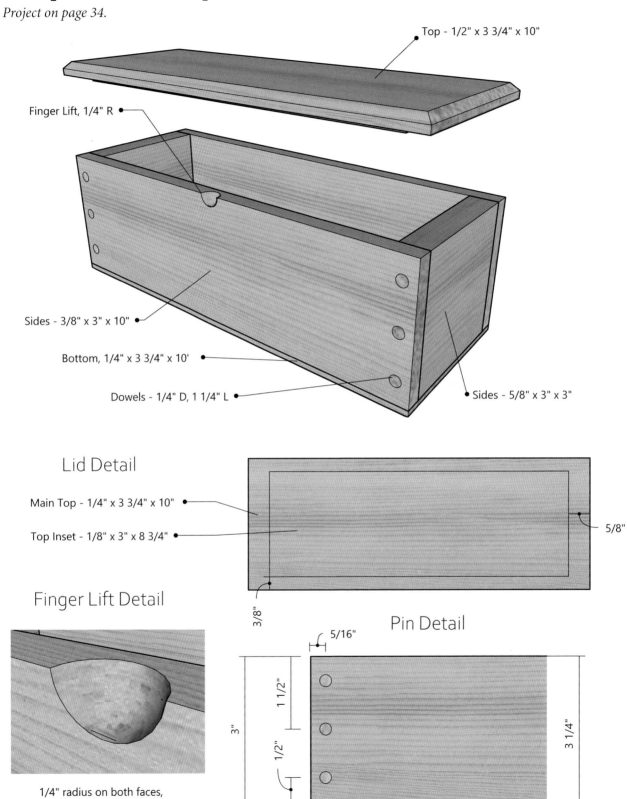

Top - 1/2" x 3 3/4" x 10"

Finger Lift, 1/4" R

Sides - 3/8" x 3" x 10"

Bottom, 1/4" x 3 3/4" x 10'

Dowels - 1/4" D, 1 1/4" L

Sides - 5/8" x 3" x 3"

Lid Detail

Main Top - 1/4" x 3 3/4" x 10"

Top Inset - 1/8" x 3" x 8 3/4"

5/8"

3/8"

Finger Lift Detail

1/4" radius on both faces,
centered on edge of box side

Pin Detail

5/16"

3"

1 1/2"

1/2"

3 1/4"

Cherry Keepsake Box

Project on page 40.

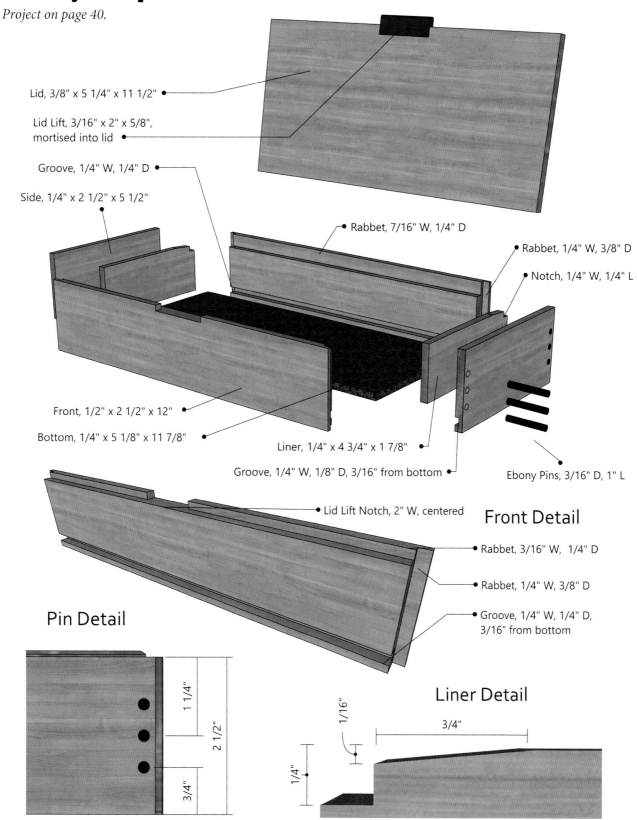

Lid, 3/8" x 5 1/4" x 11 1/2"

Lid Lift, 3/16" x 2" x 5/8", mortised into lid

Groove, 1/4" W, 1/4" D

Side, 1/4" x 2 1/2" x 5 1/2"

Rabbet, 7/16" W, 1/4" D

Rabbet, 1/4" W, 3/8" D

Notch, 1/4" W, 1/4" L

Front, 1/2" x 2 1/2" x 12"

Bottom, 1/4" x 5 1/8" x 11 7/8"

Liner, 1/4" x 4 3/4" x 1 7/8"

Groove, 1/4" W, 1/8" D, 3/16" from bottom

Ebony Pins, 3/16" D, 1" L

Lid Lift Notch, 2" W, centered

Front Detail

Rabbet, 3/16" W, 1/4" D

Rabbet, 1/4" W, 3/8" D

Groove, 1/4" W, 1/4" D, 3/16" from bottom

Pin Detail

1 1/4"

2 1/2"

3/4"

Liner Detail

1/16"

3/4"

1/4"

Bubinga Gift Box with Framed Lid

Project on page 48.

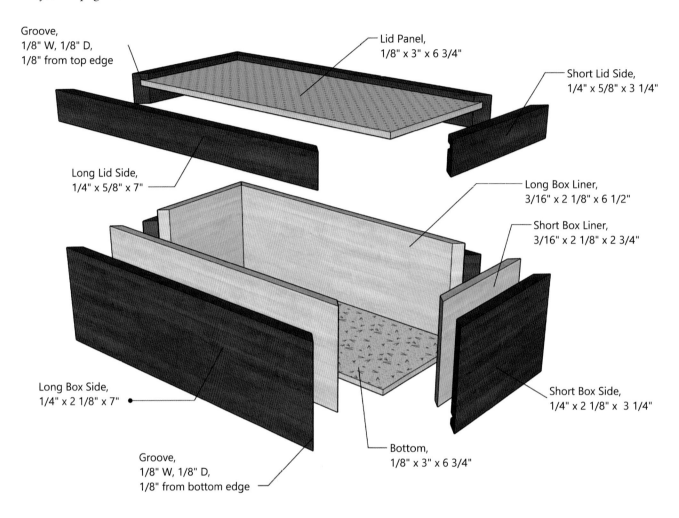

Groove,
1/8" W, 1/8" D,
1/8" from top edge

Lid Panel,
1/8" x 3" x 6 3/4"

Short Lid Side,
1/4" x 5/8" x 3 1/4"

Long Lid Side,
1/4" x 5/8" x 7"

Long Box Liner,
3/16" x 2 1/8" x 6 1/2"

Short Box Liner,
3/16" x 2 1/8" x 2 3/4"

Long Box Side,
1/4" x 2 1/8" x 7"

Short Box Side,
1/4" x 2 1/8" x 3 1/4"

Groove,
1/8" W, 1/8" D,
1/8" from bottom edge

Bottom,
1/8" x 3" x 6 3/4"

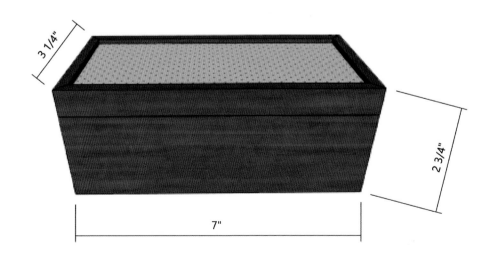

3 1/4"

2 3/4"

7"

Curly Maple Trinket Box with Ebony Pull

Project on page 54.

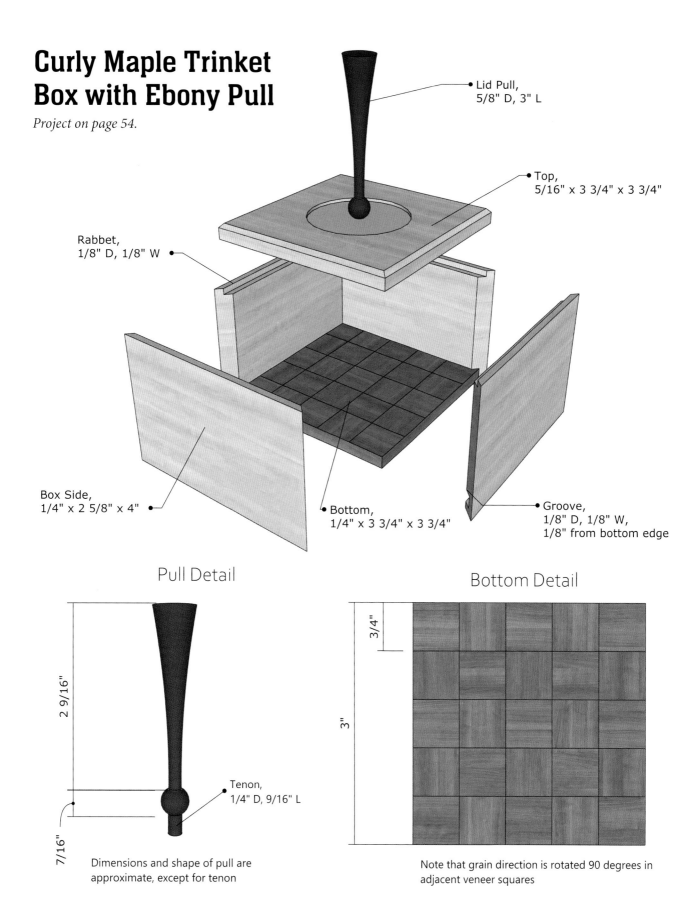

Lid Pull,
5/8" D, 3" L

Top,
5/16" x 3 3/4" x 3 3/4"

Rabbet,
1/8" D, 1/8" W

Box Side,
1/4" x 2 5/8" x 4"

Bottom,
1/4" x 3 3/4" x 3 3/4"

Groove,
1/8" D, 1/8" W,
1/8" from bottom edge

Pull Detail

2 9/16"

7/16"

Tenon,
1/4" D, 9/16" L

Dimensions and shape of pull are
approximate, except for tenon

Bottom Detail

3/4"

3"

Note that grain direction is rotated 90 degrees in
adjacent veneer squares

Salt Cellar with Finger Joints

Project on page 64.

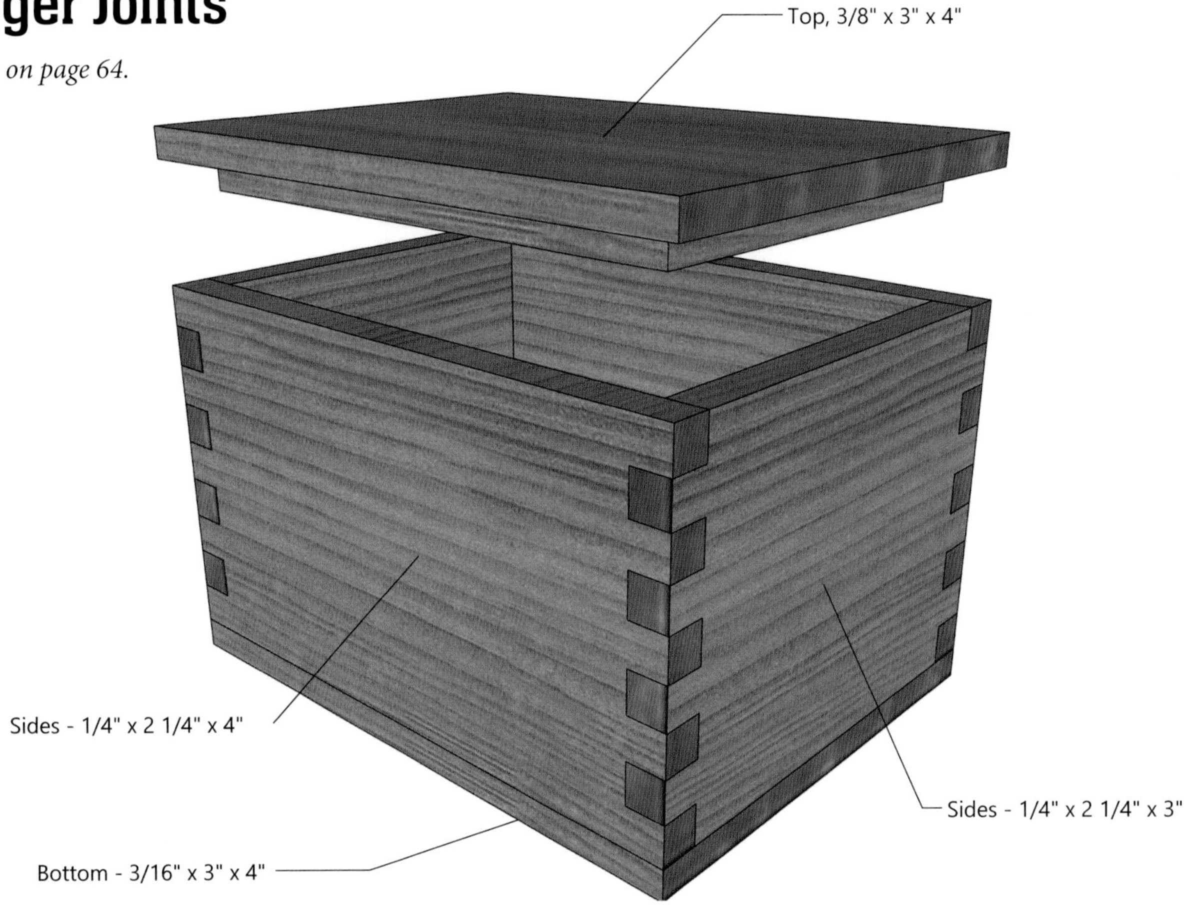

Top, 3/8" x 3" x 4"

Sides - 1/4" x 2 1/4" x 4"

Sides - 1/4" x 2 1/4" x 3"

Bottom - 3/16" x 3" x 4"

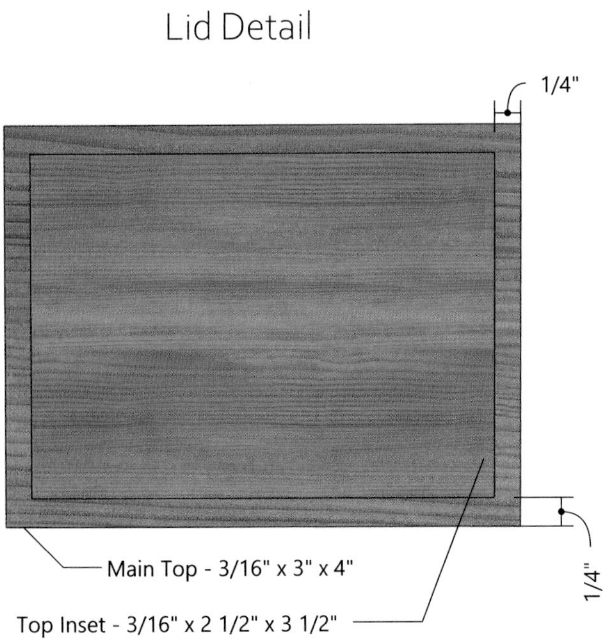

Lid Detail

1/4"

1/4"

Main Top - 3/16" x 3" x 4"

Top Inset - 3/16" x 2 1/2" x 3 1/2"

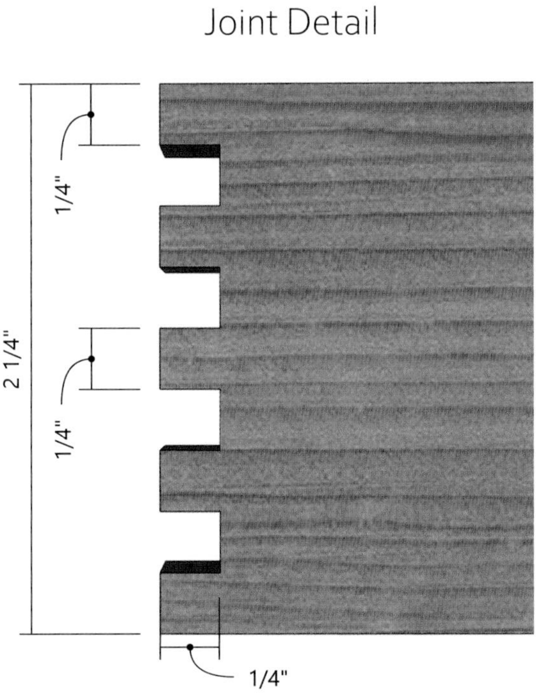

Joint Detail

1/4"

2 1/4"

1/4"

1/4"

1/4"

Two-Tone Sliding Lid Dovetail Box

Project on page 72.

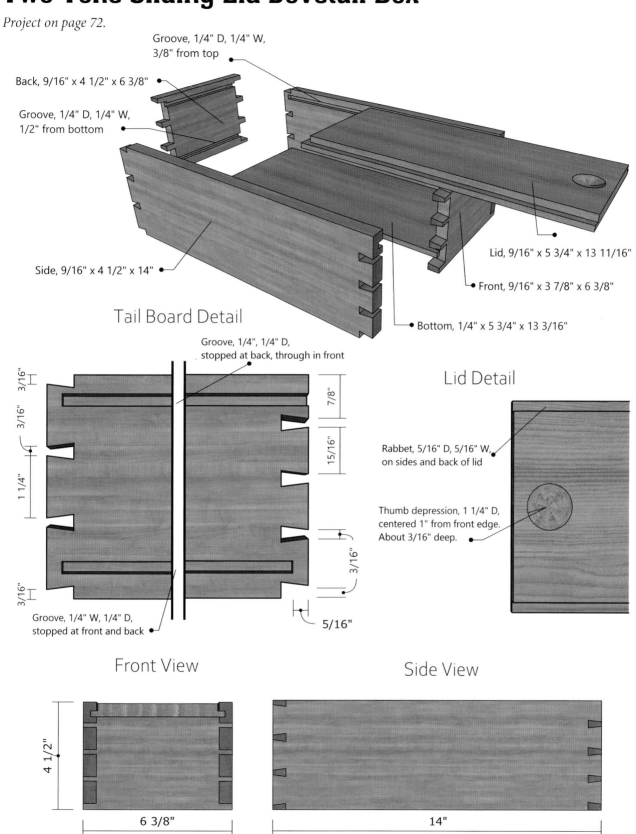

Groove, 1/4" D, 1/4" W, 3/8" from top

Back, 9/16" x 4 1/2" x 6 3/8"

Groove, 1/4" D, 1/4" W, 1/2" from bottom

Side, 9/16" x 4 1/2" x 14"

Lid, 9/16" x 5 3/4" x 13 11/16"

Front, 9/16" x 3 7/8" x 6 3/8"

Bottom, 1/4" x 5 3/4" x 13 3/16"

Tail Board Detail

Groove, 1/4", 1/4" D, stopped at back, through in front

3/16"

3/16"

3/16"

1 1/4"

3/16"

7/8"

15/16"

3/16"

5/16"

Groove, 1/4" W, 1/4" D, stopped at front and back

Lid Detail

Rabbet, 5/16" D, 5/16" W, on sides and back of lid

Thumb depression, 1 1/4" D, centered 1" from front edge. About 3/16" deep.

Front View

4 1/2"

6 3/8"

Side View

14"

Miniature Dovetailed Chest

Project on page 82.

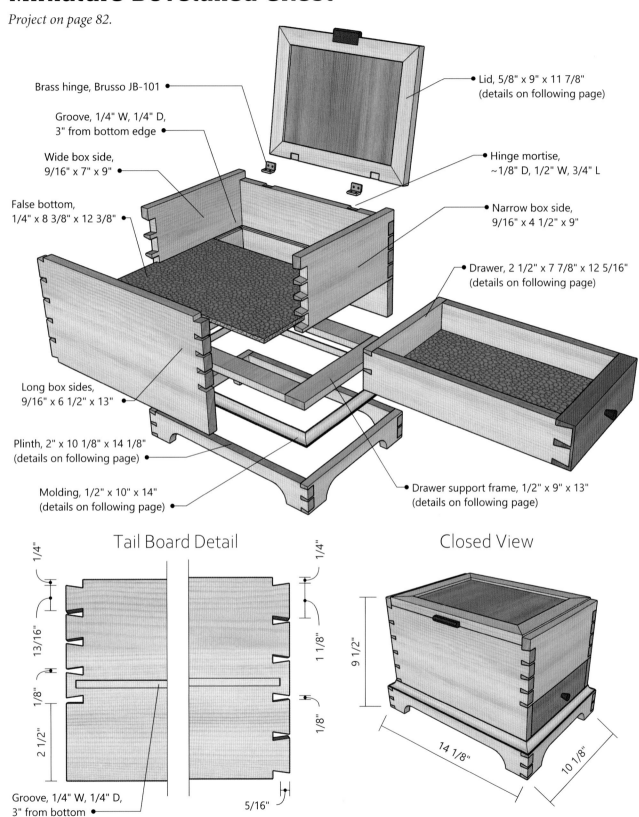

Brass hinge, Brusso JB-101

Groove, 1/4" W, 1/4" D,
3" from bottom edge

Wide box side,
9/16" x 7" x 9"

False bottom,
1/4" x 8 3/8" x 12 3/8"

Lid, 5/8" x 9" x 11 7/8"
(details on following page)

Hinge mortise,
~1/8" D, 1/2" W, 3/4" L

Narrow box side,
9/16" x 4 1/2" x 9"

Drawer, 2 1/2" x 7 7/8" x 12 5/16"
(details on following page)

Long box sides,
9/16" x 6 1/2" x 13"

Plinth, 2" x 10 1/8" x 14 1/8"
(details on following page)

Molding, 1/2" x 10" x 14"
(details on following page)

Drawer support frame, 1/2" x 9" x 13"
(details on following page)

Tail Board Detail

1/4"

1/4"

13/16"

1 1/8"

1/8"

1/8"

2 1/2"

Groove, 1/4" W, 1/4" D,
3" from bottom

5/16"

Closed View

9 1/2"

14 1/8"

10 1/8"

Miniature Dovetailed Chest
(cont.)

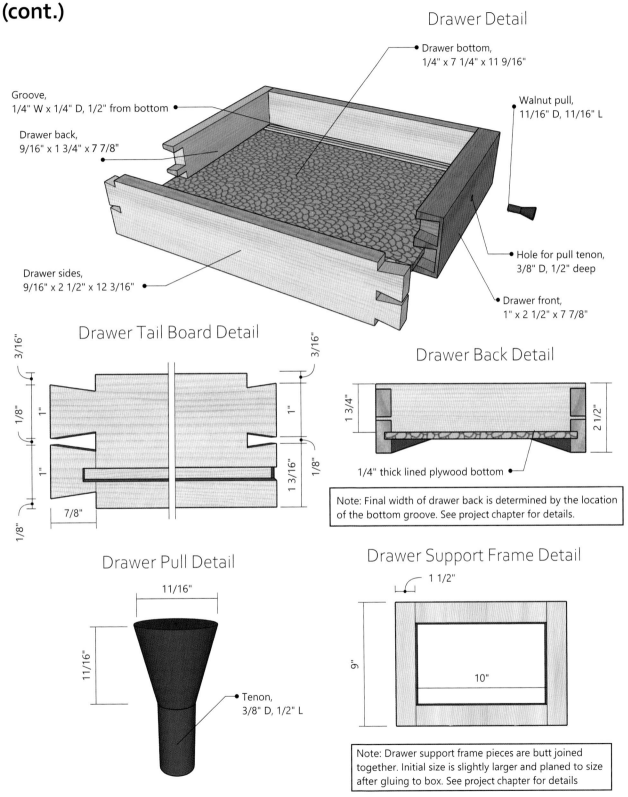

Drawer Detail

Drawer bottom,
1/4" x 7 1/4" x 11 9/16"

Groove,
1/4" W x 1/4" D, 1/2" from bottom

Walnut pull,
11/16" D, 11/16" L

Drawer back,
9/16" x 1 3/4" x 7 7/8"

Hole for pull tenon,
3/8" D, 1/2" deep

Drawer sides,
9/16" x 2 1/2" x 12 3/16"

Drawer front,
1" x 2 1/2" x 7 7/8"

Drawer Tail Board Detail

3/16"
3/16"
1/8"
1"
1"
1"
1 3/16"
1/8"
1/8"
7/8"

Drawer Back Detail

1 3/4"
2 1/2"

1/4" thick lined plywood bottom

Note: Final width of drawer back is determined by the location of the bottom groove. See project chapter for details.

Drawer Pull Detail

11/16"
11/16"

Tenon,
3/8" D, 1/2" L

Drawer Support Frame Detail

1 1/2"
9"
10"

Note: Drawer support frame pieces are butt joined together. Initial size is slightly larger and planed to size after gluing to box. See project chapter for details

Miniature Dovetailed Chest
(cont.)

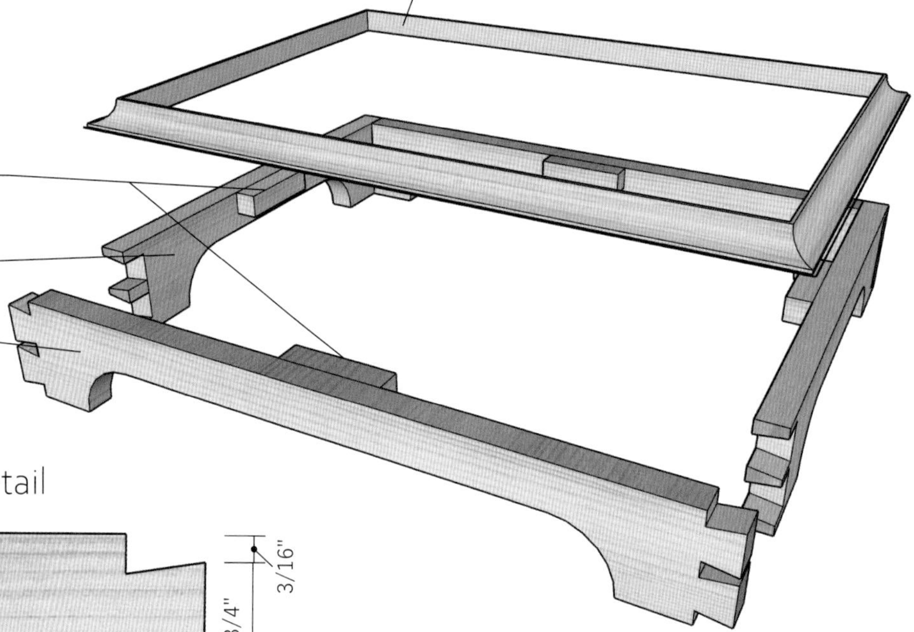

Plinth molding,
1/2" x 1/2" x 10" and 14",
four molding pieces mitered and glued to
box and plinth. Final length determined
after plinth is attached to box.

Plinth glue blocks,
1/2" x 1/2" x 2",
roughly centered on pin and
tail boards

Pin board,
9/16" x 2" x 10 1/8"

Tail board,
9/16" x 2" x 14 1/8"

Tail Board Detail

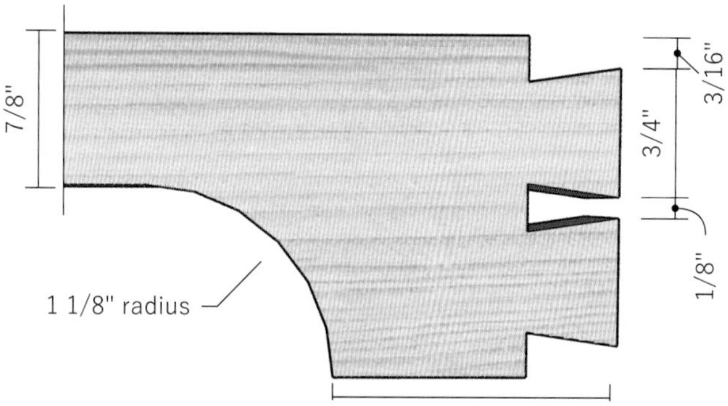

7/8"

3/16"

3/4"

1/8"

1 1/8" radius

1 3/4"

Top Detail

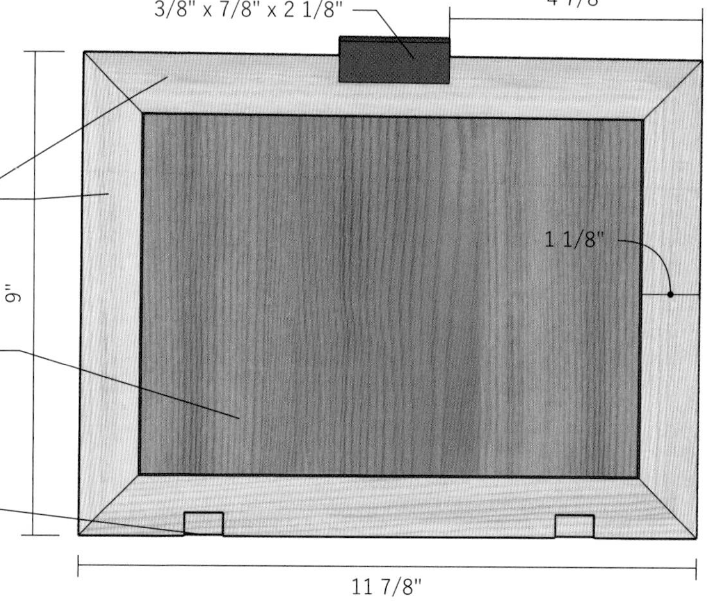

Walnut lid lift,
3/8" x 7/8" x 2 1/8"

4 7/8"

Door frame sides,
5/8" x 1 1/8" x 9" and 11 7/8",
1/4" groove 1/4" deep centered on edge.
Final length determined after box is
assembled

1 1/8"

Cherry lid panel,
1/4" x 10 1/8" x 7 1/4",
final size determined after lid
frame is sized

9"

Hinge mortise,
~1/8" D, 1/2" W, 3/4" L,
location determined after mortises
for hinges on box are cut

11 7/8"

Catchall Tray with Marquetry

Project on page 102. Marquetry pattern on page 150.

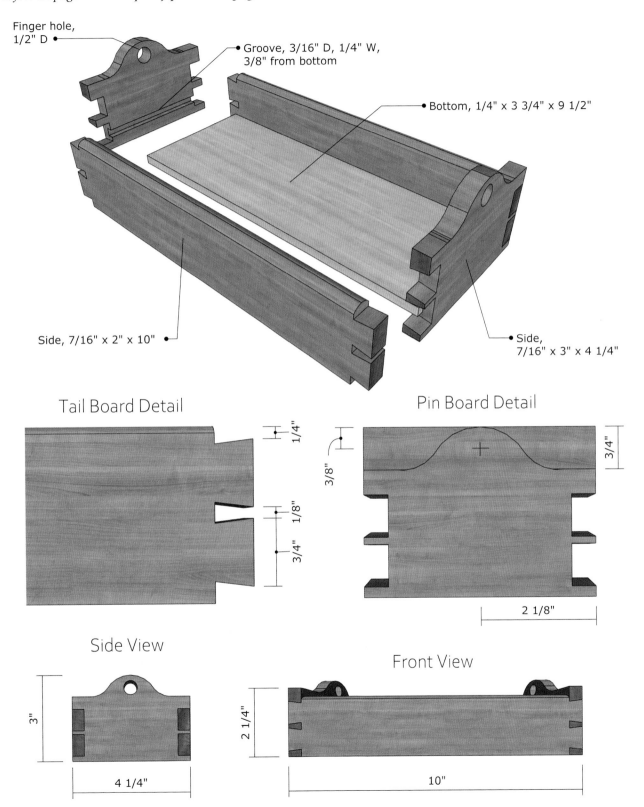

Finger hole, 1/2" D

Groove, 3/16" D, 1/4" W, 3/8" from bottom

Bottom, 1/4" x 3 3/4" x 9 1/2"

Side, 7/16" x 2" x 10"

Side, 7/16" x 3" x 4 1/4"

Tail Board Detail

1/4"

1/8"

3/4"

Pin Board Detail

3/4"

3/8"

2 1/8"

Side View

3"

4 1/4"

Front View

2 1/4"

10"

Assymmetrical Band Saw Box

Project on page 114.

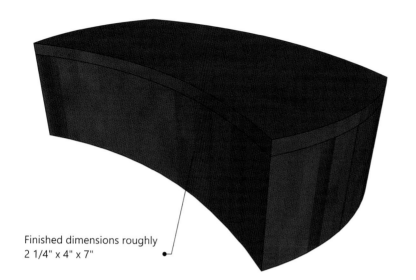

Box exterior is shaped freeform after assembly -- this final shape follows the example in the project chapter. Final shape can vary, but all instructions and critical dimensions are based on starting with a 2 1/2" thick, 7 1/2" long, and 4 1/4" wide solid wood blank.

Finished dimensions roughly 2 1/4" x 4" x 7"

Interior Detail

Interior sides are sloped inward by tilting band saw table.

Lid Detail

Lid inset is cut from the interior waste of the box, so the sides follow the interior slope

Marking the Blank

Use the diagram on the right to mark the endgrain of your box blank. Don't worry too much about being extra precise here—as long as you don't stray too much from the listed dimensions, everything will be fine.

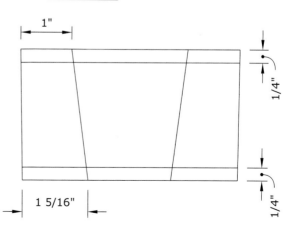

1"

1/4"

1/4"

1 5/16"

Padauk and Curly Maple Turned Ring Box

Project on page 120.

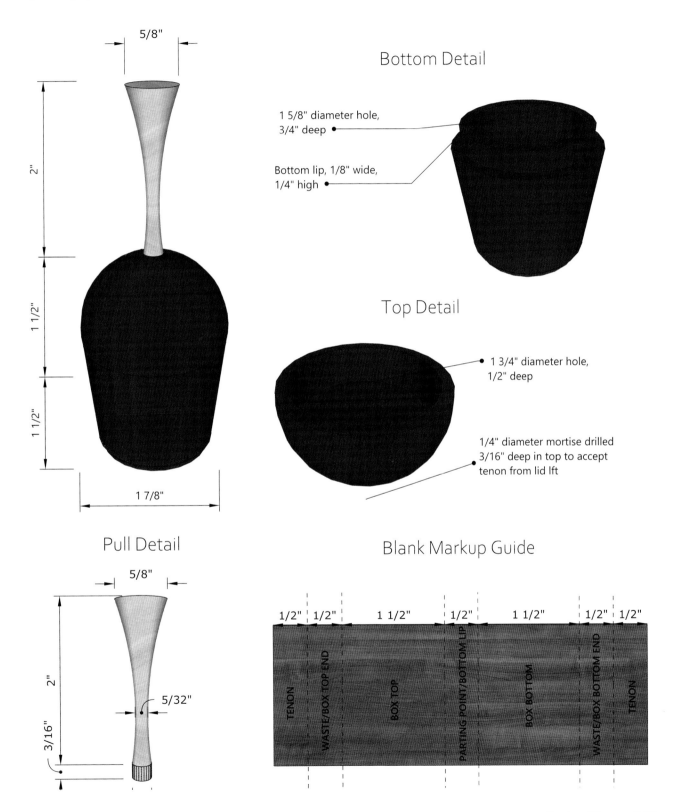

5/8"

2"

1 1/2"

1 1/2"

1 7/8"

Bottom Detail

1 5/8" diameter hole, 3/4" deep

Bottom lip, 1/8" wide, 1/4" high

Top Detail

1 3/4" diameter hole, 1/2" deep

1/4" diameter mortise drilled 3/16" deep in top to accept tenon from lid lft

Pull Detail

5/8"

2"

5/32"

3/16"

Blank Markup Guide

1/2"   1/2"   1 1/2"   1/2"   1 1/2"   1/2"   1/2"

TENON

WASTE/BOX TOP END

BOX TOP

PARTING POINT/BOTTOM LIP

BOX BOTTOM

WASTE/BOX BOTTOM END

TENON

Catchall Tray with Marquetry, Pattern

Project on page 102.

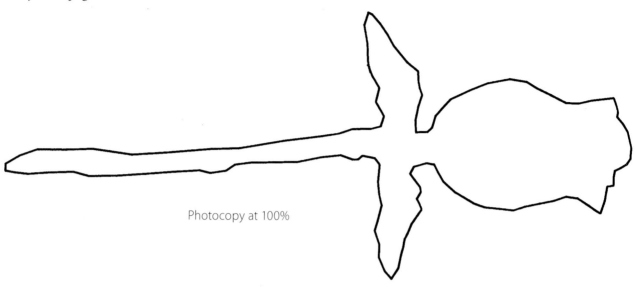

Photocopy at 100%

About the Author

Albert Kleine is a self-taught hobbyist woodworker based out of a small shed in suburban Washington, D.C. Over the past decade, he has focused heavily on fine box-making, more recently delving into carving, marquetry, and other decorative aspects of woodworking. He teaches both in-person and virtually, and plans on expanding classes to his home shop in the near future. His work has been featured in multiple publications, such as *Fine Woodworking and Popular Woodworking*. Outside of woodworking, Albert is an economist at his day job and the proud father of Maximilian.

Index

Note: Page numbers in *italics* indicate images.
Page numbers in **bold** indicate project plans.